IN WESTERN CANADA
BEFORE THE WAR

Other SPECTRA titles

North-West of Sixteen
                    J. G. MacGregor
The Boy in Buckskins
                         Iris Allan
The Emperor of Peace River
                    Eugenie Louise Myles
Between the Red and the Rockies
                    Grant MacEwan

IN WESTERN CANADA BEFORE THE WAR

IMPRESSIONS OF EARLY TWENTIETH CENTURY PRAIRIE COMMUNITIES

Elizabeth B. Mitchell

with an introduction by Susan Jackel

Western Producer Prairie Books
Saskatoon, Saskatchewan

Copyright © 1981 by the estate of E. B. Mitchell
Western Producer Prairie Books
Saskatoon, Saskatchewan

First published by John Murray, London, in 1915
This SPECTRA edition by Western Producer Prairie Books in 1981

Cover photo by permission of Provincial Museum and Archives of Alberta

Printed and bound in Canada
by
Modern Press
Saskatoon, Saskatchewan

Western Producer Prairie Book publications are produced and manufactured in the middle of Western Canada by a unique publishing venture owned by a group of prairie farmers who are members of Saskatchewan Wheat Pool. From the first book published in 1954, a reprint of a serial originally carried in the weekly newspaper, *The Western Producer*, to the book before you now, the tradition of providing enjoyable and informative reading for all Canadians is continued.

Canadian Cataloguing in Publication Data
Mitchell, Elizabeth B. (Elizabeth Buchanan), 1880-1980.
    In Western Canada before the war

    (Spectra series)
    First published: London : J. Murray, 1915.
    ISBN 0-88833-069-3

    1. Prairie Provinces — Description and travel —
1905-1950.* 2. Prairie Provinces — Social
conditions.* 3. Cities and towns — Prairie
Provinces. I. Title. II. Series.
    FC3242.M57 1981   971.2'02   C81-091174-4
    F1060.9.M57 1981

To the kindest of cousins,
who first received me into
a North-Western home

CONTENTS

Acknowledgements to the SPECTRA Introduction

My thanks go to Beatrice Parlby for her help in tracking down the little-known author of *In Western Canada Before the War*. It was a chance remark of hers, about "the year Miss Mitchell came to Alix," that set me on the trail to the Town and Country Planning Association in London, which kindly supplied a copy of *The Plan That Pleased*, the source of the biographical material on Mitchell in the introduction. From there the trail led to the East Kilbride Development Corporation in Glasgow, and then to Elizabeth Mitchell herself at her home in Stirling. The revelation that Mitchell was still alive and well, sixty-five years after the original publication of her book, lent extra interest and urgency to the preparation of this reprint, and the news of her death last July was received with regret.

Susan Jackel

INTRODUCTION TO THE SPECTRA EDITION

In Western Canada Before the War was first published in 1915 by the London firm of John Murray. At first glance it seems to fall readily into a category of prose writing widely practised in the century's early years, namely the British book of travel to the outer reaches of the Empire. Members of Britain's reading public were very interested in the colonies, chiefly because many turn-of-the-century Britons had either half-formed thoughts of emigrating, or friends and relatives who had already done so. Thus, between 1880 and 1914 a steady stream of travel accounts were published in London, as footloose journalists and gentlefolk wrote up their tours of America or New Zealand or South Africa or Canada where millions of expatriate Britons were engaged in building new societies.

Few of the authors of these volumes of travel and comment expected to produce books of lasting value; nor, as a rule, did they succeed in doing so. Working on the assumption that their readers in Britain wanted to be mildly amused, painlessly informed, they wrote to address current interests and to reach as wide a market as possible. Under these circumstances, to offer anything so strenuous as a "study" was to take a considerable risk.

But Elizabeth Mitchell was neither tourist nor journalist, and she took that risk. Herself "a student of the growth of institutions," (her own phrase), Mitchell wrote principally for those who shared her absorption in the problems and possibilities of modern industrial society. The subtitle of the original 1915 edition, "A Study of Communities," gave a clear indication of her serious intent. Yet in manner and tone her writing is anything but ponderous, and through it both scholar and general reader can form a picture of the prairie provinces of Canada as they appeared to a singularly thoughtful and perceptive observer on the eve of the first world war. As a result, Elizabeth Mitchell's "short account of what I had seen and guessed among the rising communities of the prairies" stands well above the general level of travel writing. It seems unlikely there will be many to quarrel with Kenneth McNaught's judgement that *In Western Canada Before the War* remains "one of the best contemporary foreign books about Canada" to appear during the years of western settlement.

Elizabeth Mitchell was born on 21 July 1880, into a comfortable Edinburgh home. Her father, an advocate and later Sheriff-Substitute of Stirling, had spent his student days at Oxford, where he met with and absorbed the ideas of William Morris. Edinburgh in the 1880s was a centre of lively intellectual debate, and a frequent topic of discussion in the Mitchell household was Patrick Geddes and his experiments in housing reform in Edinburgh's older quarters. The young Elizabeth attended St. George's School for Girls in Edinburgh; then, in her early twenties she enrolled at Oxford in classical Mods and Greats, the most arduous and therefore the most respected course of study in the University. She completed the course with first class honours, one of a handful of women to achieve this distinction before World War I.

It was while she was at Oxford that Elizabeth Mitchell came into contact with the ideas of the fledgling Garden Cities movement, and her record of that decisive encounter is worth quoting (it comes from her autobiography, *The Plan That Pleased*, published in 1967):

> One day in 1906 a vigorous young woman came to lunch. Sybella Burney . . . had a story to pour into [our] ears. A London law-reporter, Ebenezer Howard, had written a book and said that this present endless spread of London, with all its horrible rush-hours and monotonous suburbs, was just nonsense; and that the thing to do was to stop the shapeless endless sprawl and start new towns well out beyond a green belt. Towns, observe, not suburbs each of one kind of thing. Towns, with all proper variety, with work and houses and churches and recreation, all planned for human beings.
> . . . Naturally I cocked my ears. Here was a man who not only thought that something was fundamentally wrong with most of our modern towns, but thought something could be done about it. And here were people actually setting out to try. I was not at that time in a position to invest in the development of Letchworth, but I could join

the propagandist Garden Cities Association (later
the Town and Country Planning Association) and
so I did (pp. 4-5).

The activities of the Town and Country
Planning Association were to dominate the rest of
Elizabeth Mitchell's long and eventful lifetime.
Guided by the ideas of such pioneers in community planning as Ebenezer Howard, Raymond
Unwin, and Thomas Adams, this association was
formed principally to combat the intensifying
concentration of Britain's industrial population
into great urban centres. Its members argued that
the best way to alleviate the overcrowding and
wastefulness of uncontrolled city growth was to
create new towns of moderate size, complete with
industry, services, and all the amenities of truly
civilized urban life. Surrounding green-belts for
recreation, and farms that would ensure a nearby
supply of food were to be included in these
amenities. Nor were the proponents of new towns
content to confine their energies to argument. The
town of Letchworth, founded in 1903 thirty-five
miles north of London, became the tangible
embodiment of Ebenezer Howard's visionary
schemes. Its successor, Welwyn Garden City, was
established immediately after World War I. Together, these experiments helped to encourage
supporters of the new towns movement to believe
that solutions to some of Britain's most pressing
social problems lay at hand.

Throughout the inter-war years the English
cities of London, Manchester, and Liverpool
seemed to present the most urgent cases for action.

In the mining and industrial north, however, the twin problems of rural depopulation and urban congestion were no less acute. The city of Glasgow, in fact, had density rates more than double those of Liverpool; in certain working-class districts, the crumbling stone tenements housed as many as seven hundred people to the acre. Small-scale remedies of the kind carried out by Patrick Geddes in Edinburgh half a century before were clearly inadequate; more drastic measures were required without delay. In *The Plan That Pleased*, her book of memoirs, Elizabeth Mitchell recorded how the principles of town and country planning came to Scotland:

> A few leaders, including Sir William Whyte of Lanarkshire, Frank Preston of Milngavie, and Jean Mann of Glasgow, had moved forward from the terrible problems of overcrowding to the revolutionary idea that the long-continued drift of population towards the congested centres was not after all an eternal immutable law of nature. Might it in fact be a historical process which had gone beyond what was humanly right and practical? Ought it, could it perhaps be stopped and even reversed by dispersal to smaller roomier towns, each with a life of its own? . . . The cure could not be found by the local authorities acting independently of one another. There must be co-operation to bring together somehow the congestion here and the depopulation there. Sir William Whyte led in the call for a national plan for Scotland (pp. 22-23).

So, in 1937 the Scottish Branch of the Town and Country Planning Association was born, with

Elizabeth Mitchell as secretary and soon as chairman of the executive.

For the second time in a generation, the implementation of policies directed against Britain's urban problems was prevented by the outbreak of war; yet the incursions of German bombers proved to be decisive in the end. The destruction in English cities during World War II ensured that housing would become a top priority in the plans of post-war British governments, and throughout the United Kingdom the changing political climate favoured the initiatives of the new towns movement.

Town and country planning was not the only cause to which Elizabeth Mitchell devoted herself during those years. For much of World War I she served as honorary secretary to a volunteer committee engaged in drawing women into agriculture, in an experiment which foreshadowed the Women's Land Army of World War II. At the war's end, this group became an official board of enquiry into the position of women in agriculture in Scotland. Mitchell was also instrumental in bringing Women's Institutes to rural Scotland. In her memoirs she recounts how, towards the end of World War I, she was called on to describe "what I had seen of the home-makers in Saskatchewan and the country-women's clubs in Alberta." Her description convinced dubious parish leaders in Lanarkshire that what was working so well in Canada could improve the quality of life for Scottish women as well.

After the war Mitchell went on to play an even
more active part in public life. Throughout the
1920s she sat as an elected member of the
education authority of the County of Lanark, and
also helped to set up the county's circulating
library. Mitchell even tried her hand at national
politics, standing as a Liberal candidate for Parliament in 1924 and again in 1929. Both times she lost
her deposit, but she believed that the experience
she gained, made these attempts worthwhile.
Moreover, she had the satisfaction of knowing that
once again she had been a pioneer and in a cause
that was especially close to her heart, for as she
explained in her memoirs, "I was the first woman
candidate in Lanarkshire, the defeated forerunner
of a strong successful band — Jenny Lee, Helen
Shaw, Margaret Herbison, Jean Mann, Judith
Hart" (p. 16).

From 1929 onwards, however, the overriding
interest in Elizabeth Mitchell's life was housing
reform in Scotland. For more than thirty years she
was a mainstay of the new towns movement there.
Working entirely as a volunteer, she addressed
meetings, served on councils, formulated propos-
als, and wrote numerous articles for planning
journals and other publications. "We were distinc-
tively a propagandist society," she later wrote of
the TCPA's role in Scotland in the 1930s and '40s.
The process of public education was slow, but she
kept at it with a patience and good humour that
won the respect and friendship of all who knew
her. Finally success came with the designation in
1946 of East Kilbride as the first of the Scottish

new towns, followed by Glenrothes in 1948 and Cumbernauld in 1956. Public recognition of Elizabeth Mitchell's many services to the people of Scotland finally came too when, on 2 December 1955 Mitchell was awarded the Ebenezer Howard Memorial Medal at a special dinner held in her honour in the House of Commons at Westminster.

Although the events of the mid-1950s probably marked the high point of Elizabeth Mitchell's life, there were many busy and useful years ahead of her. She continued her work for the Scottish TCPA until a brief illness in 1962 suggested the wisdom of retirement (she was then eighty-one). She spent the next few years writing her memoirs, which she intended principally to be a contribution to the history of town and country planning in Britain. Like all of her writing, this sixty-page document gives abundant evidence of a firm, clear mind, one undiminished in vigour despite its author's eighty-seven years.

It therefore seems an act of natural justice that Elizabeth Mitchell should have retained full use of her faculties until close to her very recent death. According to her housekeeper, Mitchell's memory began to fail somewhat after she fell and broke her leg in 1978; nevertheless an operation enabled her to walk again, and her sight, hearing and general health remained unimpaired. When she was informed in the spring of 1980 that *In Western Canada Before the War* was being proposed for reprinting in Canada, Elizabeth Mitchell expressed her pleasure in knowing that her book of 1915 "still exists after all these years." Unfortunately she did not live to see its re-issue. She died in Stirling, Scotland on 21 July 1980, in the early hours of her one-hundredth birthday.

Elizabeth Mitchell's visit to Canada was a brief but important interlude in her exceptionally long life. She arrived in May 1913 on the day that set a new record for immigrant arrivals into this country. She returned to Scotland in the following April, having stayed nearly a year, and she began immediately to set her impressions down on paper. All but the final paragraph of *In Western Canada Before the War* was written in May and June 1914, only weeks before the outbreak of war.

Rather than offering a personal narrative of travel and experience, Mitchell undertook to provide British readers with an analysis of the underlying structures of western Canadian society. Consequently, she deliberately provided few details of the circumstances surrounding her sojourn in Canada, even going so far as to mask the identity of the Saskatchewan town she stayed in by calling it M------. In her autobiography she had no reason for wanting to suppress facts of a personal nature. Four pages of *The Plan That Pleased* deal with her year in Canada. It seems worth quoting these pages here, because they offer useful details of persons and places omitted from the book of 1915. Furthermore, they provide an excellent summary of Elizabeth Mitchell's chief conclusions about town and country life on the prairies as she had known it more than fifty years before. From Elizabeth Mitchell's autobiography, then, comes this chapter entitled "Saskalta":

So far, my life had passed for the most part in two famous cities and in the gentle landscape of South England. I had been an interested observer of communities and their surroundings, acting and re-acting on one another. From 1913 onwards the scenes were different; and here and there, little by little, I began to meddle.

In April of that year I found myself settled for some months in Western Canada in the neat new home of my enterprising cousin, Miss Lilias Mitchell, honorary deaconess in the diocese of Saskatchewan. She was stationed at North Battleford.

North Battleford was a town somewhere about seven years old, sprung up when the Canadian Northern Railway came through and a wide district of open prairie was allocated for settlement, in square plots of 160 acres, "quarters" of a square mile. The town was basically a creation of the railway; it was growing every day. Old Battleford, in contrast, was an almost venerable group of buildings on the far side of the North Saskatchewan valley. It dated from fur-trading and ranching days; it contained the Court House and the Mounted Police Barracks, and was the scene in early summer of an annual rally of Indians. My cousin was interested in Old Battleford with its old traditions, but young North Battleford had her heart.

First impressions were surprising and happy. It was a marvel to see so much accomplished in so few years, such a bright town; clean and tidy except at the edges, orderly in conduct. (The police and the Court House deserved great credit.)

The original mud had been countered by wooden side-walks, and an effective water-supply had been brought in a year or two ago—my cousin said she dated civilization from that point. I realized something of what water meant in a wooden town when the fire-alarm went one evening during a town meeting, and every man instantly leapt to his feet and dashed to the scene with the urgency of earlier days.

All along the railway across three provinces, in those pre-1914 days, new towns were bursting up from the empty prairie like the grass and flowers after the thaw. The air was full of youth and confidence. The citizens were so proud of their towns, partly no doubt from the profit motive, partly from sheer exuberance. It was a refreshing atmosphere to breathe.

In Britain, in those days, "new town" was almost an improper word, a shocking visionary idea, though, after all, even there all the towns had been new once, and Birmingham and Motherwell not so very long ago. But in Western Canada new towns were going up by dozens, and I had the chance of seeing the process actually going on. What were the prospects? How far were the busy, happy, zestful creators guarding against return of the old troubles?

They were certainly guarding against one nineteenth-century mistake. The towns were not shapeless, they had a plan firmly imposed. Unfortunately it was a poor plan, a rigid grid-iron. (That was fifty years ago, times have changed.) The grid plan was easy to apply, as the site was nearly level, but how dull it was, what a waste of opportunity! Where was the market-place or piazza, to unite the citizens? Where could you place a fine building so that it could be properly seen as the culmination of a vista along the street, like St. George's dome in Edinburgh? Every street went on and on till it expired in an indefinite end. Roman Catholic authorities have generally a good eye for a site (perhaps from a Mediterranean tradition?) but even they had not managed in my time at North Battleford to set a church across a street for the eye to rest on. (I am interested to learn that they have now planted a great institution on a fine site in a new, well-designed quarter of the city.) Fifty years ago the best an ambitious builder could hope for was a corner site, how poor compared with an open space, even a small one. The traffic troubles of a grid were not then serious, as it was the age of wagons and buggies, and the streets were wide.

So, to sum up first impressions, the confidence and determination were splendid, and there was a layout plan, but the plan was poor. Were there slums? Not isolated by themselves. There was ample air and light for everybody. The citizens were generally on easy terms with one another. There was untidiness on the outskirts and a tendency towards a superior attitude north of the railway, but there was not yet a hard obvious segregation.

Dimly, as the weeks went on, I began to feel that there was in fact a social cleavage, rather unexpected. The economic function of the town was in the first place as a main station on the railway, with marshalling-yards and repair shops; and the economic function of that was to serve the homesteaders in the district around by supplying their needs from the outer world and sending off their wheat on its long journey to Britain. The basic function was like that of an old market-town on a coach road, but the atmosphere was different. The farmers did not seem to dominate the scene as on a market-day in an old country town. The men who were breaking the soil seemed to slip in separately and half-shyly and to feel rather out of place in their rough clothes. The talk of the town was not so much of methods of pioneer farming as of the soaring price of town lots. At that time of boom, the most moneyed citizens were those who had speculated most successfully in real-estate values. The homesteader was a poor chap who had not had the wits to do better.

My cousin's work gave her a special position as between town and country. For one thing, she gave hospitality from time to time to the young unmarried clergy of the diocese who were stationed in rude simplicity far out on the prairie. For another, if a bride-to-be arrived from Europe on the station platform one uncertain day to marry a young man wrestling far out to break the ground and build a home—he might not be waiting on the platform to receive her and there was then no rural telephone to reach him. The railwaymen used to send the girl up to Miss Mitchell—"She'll see you through". A day or two later the young man would turn up, Miss Mitchell would act mother to the bride, and send the couple off with a promise to visit them before the summer was over. So we visited some primitive homes and saw something of the fierce hard work and the loneliness, also something of the grand spaces of the sunlit prairie and the grand people forged by the hard conditions, while others proved unequal to the test.

Out there we came on traces of an extraordinarily valuable influence. There were clubs beginning, the Grain-growers and the Home-makers. They met monthly or fortnightly in the little prairie school. The strong old pioneers could pass on all sorts of knowledge and comfort to despairing young ones. Everybody could enjoy seeing other people after the loneliness and the distances. The provincial authorities, we found, and especially the University of Saskatoon, were encouraging these clubs with all their might, as meeting an enormous want. The homesteaders were so lonely and unorganized. They came from all sorts of backgrounds: townsmen, countrymen, Ukrainian peasants, Scottish crofters, English gentry, as well as the Eastern Canadians and Middle-West Americans who understood the conditions best. The distances were sometimes increased by sad derelict "quarters" abandoned to the gophers and the weeds.

The "rurals" in Scotland and the women's institutes in England have done good work; on the prairie, where the newcomers knew nobody, the value of the rural clubs was unspeakably great. One of the real prides of my life is that near the end of my year in Canada, at Alix, Alberta, I talked so much to my hostess—a dominant woman—about the homemakers' club in Saskatchewan that she dragged me out in an open sledge in 50° of frost to talk to some neighbour women—and the Countrywomen's Club of Alix was founded. I had a letter lately from Alix asking me for some memories of the occasion because the club had lost its records in a fire.

While recalling these prairie memories I felt it would be interesting to have news of North Battleford after fifty years. It is a city now and an important nodal point in the national road system. With its countryside, it came through the sorrows of the 'thirties and has emerged as the prosperous centre of a mixed-farming district worked in larger units than the old 160 acres. The faith and hope of the pioneers have been justified.

M------, then, was North Battleford, and "the kindest of cousins" to whom this book was originally dedicated was Lilias Mitchell, Anglican deaconess and friend to stranded brides. The closing paragraphs of this later account also reveal that Elizabeth Mitchell was more than simply an observer of western Canada's social development, she was an active participant as well. Her role was small, but it was not inconsequential, since it was she who provided the initial impetus to organization among the farm women of Alberta.

In Western Canada Before the War alludes to this episode in the remark on page 41: "I was very proud later when in a certain district of Alberta a Country-women's Club was formed partly because I had talked so much about the Home-makers of Saskatchewan." What her memoirs tell us is that the "certain district" was none other than Alix, Alberta, home of the Parlby family and birthplace of the United Farm Women of Alberta. Mitchell's hostess during her visit to Alix in that frosty January of 1914 was Jean C. Reed who, in addition to being an ardent suffragist and a long-time friend of the Pankhursts, was also housekeeper-companion to Sheila Marryat, the sister of Irene Parlby. In *Pioneers and Progress*, a local history of the Alix-Clive district, Beatrice Parlby describes the sequence of events that followed Elizabeth Mitchell's stay in Alix:

Miss Mitchell had just visited friends in Saskatchewan where she had been taken to a meeting of the Homemakers' Club. She was so delighted with the very businesslike way those women conducted their meeting that she described it all to Jean Reed and to everyone else who would listen. Scarcely a month later, a meeting of the women of rural Alix was called in the Anglican Rectory, and a Country Women's Club was organized with Mrs. R. W. (Leona) Barritt as President and Irene Parlby as Secretary-Treasurer.

The next January (1915) Mr. Woodbridge of the United Farmers of Alberta invited them to the men's annual meeting in Calgary and this club, with women from other areas, formed a Women's Auxiliary to the U.F.A. Several delegates went from Alix ... The following year, 1916, Irene Parlby was elected Provincial President, and under her leadership the women's organization became the United Farm Women of Alberta, instead of just an auxiliary. The little club at Alix became U.F.W.A. Local No. 1.

... The little club gave women their first chance to get together to discuss their common interests and problems. This was a great training ground in public speaking and in the conducting of business. Above all it was a great step in overcoming the isolation and loneliness of a pioneer land.

Events quickly proved the value of these organizations as training grounds for the entry of Alberta women into public life. In the Alberta

provincial election of 1917 two women candidates
were elected to the legislature, and in 1921 Irene
Parlby, M.L.A. for Lacombe, was appointed Minister without Portfolio in the United Farmers of
Alberta government formed that year, a post she
held for the next fourteen years.

On the other side of that same legislature, as it
happens, sat another well-known woman politician, Nellie McClung, who was Liberal M.L.A. for
Edmonton from 1921 to 1926. In her autobiography McClung drew particular attention to the
contributions made by the province's farm women
to affairs of the day, and she arrived at the same
high estimate of their abilities that Elizabeth
Mitchell recorded in her book of 1915. The
contrast between city and country women that
Mitchell describes on pp. 51-53 of this book, may
be compared to this passage from *The Stream Runs
Fast*, the second of Nellie McClung's two autobio-
graphical volumes:

> The rural women of Alberta were the white hope
> of the progressive movement in that province. The
> Women's Institutes and United Farm Women
> were not afraid to tackle social problems and their
> reading courses and discussions showed serious
> purpose. The women of the cities were more likely
> to be entangled in social affairs and in danger of
> wasting their time in matters of constitution and
> procedure, such as "Who should sit at the head
> table at their annual banquet?" but there was real
> stuff in the countrywomen.

Coming to Canada from the United Kingdom,
where the suffrage campaign extended over a long

period of time and was bitterly fought, Elizabeth Mitchell was naturally impressed by the atmosphere of relative reason and goodwill surrounding the issue of votes for women in the western provinces. She wrote in her book (p. 56): "The most interesting suffragists are the prairie women. They have good minds, and they are accustomed to be serious, and they do think about these things, and so there is a very noticeable movement on the prairie, quite free from any exasperation at all, and quite likely, I think, to succeed soon." And succeed it did—the legislatures of all three prairie provinces extended the provincial franchise to women in the early months of 1916, with virtually none of the violence and rancour that marked the English and American movements.

Rural clubs and suffrage are only two of many topics likely to interest the modern reader of this book; Mitchell's coverage of the social scene in the pre-war prairie provinces was extensive. As a person who had been attracted since student days to the then young discipline of sociology, she naturally enquired closely into Saskatchewan's institutional life—its schools, universities, churches and charities. The reader will also find comments on western towns and cities, immigration and tight money (Mitchell was in Canada just as the great settlement boom was faltering), and an extremely thought-provoking chapter describing Canada's social structure which she called "The Great Divide." Her perceptive and informed observations on all these important issues are couched in the clear, graceful prose that points unmistakeably to Mitchell's Oxford training in classical languages and philosophy.

These chapters are balanced by others on country scenes and conditions. In them, Mitchell made very plain her sympathy for the farm people of the west and her regret that Canadians, who often boasted of their immunity to Old Country notions of class distinction, should be slipping unawares into their own home-bred form of snobbery. "There is commonly to be found, in Canadian towns and in some books, a tendency to personal deprecation of the farmer class, which is, so far as my experience goes, totally unjustified," she wrote, expressing her fear of the long-term effects of such attitudes on Canada's social cohesion. Even ethnic differences, she thought, posed less threat to the country's future than the cleavage between city dwellers and rural people: "The division of French and English has been troublesome enough to Canadian statesmen, but the breach between town and country is perhaps an even graver matter" (pp. 104-5).

Of continuing interest are her views on the groundswell of agrarian radicalism then forming in the west. It did not take her long to discern that doctrines taken very much for granted in the Scottish mining and shipbuilding districts she came from seemed strange and foreign to the majority of Canadians, particularly to those in power. On pages 202-3 below, she mentions the alarm created by "the Socialist bogey" in small western towns and among the residents of "strenuously Conservative" Ontario. Yet, as her writing

makes clear, she did not share this feeling. There is
a fine even-handed irony in her observation that
"(Church of England) catechists in the country
were horribly bothered by extreme anti-everything
Socialist views among farmers . . ." The same
skeptical tone governs her description of a stock-
producers' meeting that, contrary to the intent of
its city businessmen sponsors, "could not be kept
to the discussion of pedigree hogs, and instead
exploded like a mine with startling views on
Capitalism and the Rights of Labour."

Mitchell's incipient radicalism achieved its
sharpest focus in her two chapters on western
urban life, where she undertook to dissect the
internal and external relations of town and
country. Her attack on the speculative spirit
infecting urban development in Canada was—and
is—far from unique. It seems safe to predict that
many students of Canadian social and economic
matters, especially those acquainted with James
Lorimer's *The Developers,* will read these chapters
with a profound sense of *déjà vu.* Mitchell claimed
no particular credit personally for the clarity of her
insight into the foundations of western development. "There is a direct and deadly plainness
about some things out West," she wrote, "with no
fogging or blurring by habit and use and customary right, and the need of a stronger communal
control of town-land is one of these things. The
arguments are written in huge glaring letters right
across the prairie" (p. 128).

Once again, the reader may discern the influence of Mitchell's Oxford background, indissol-

ubly interwoven with the philosophy of the Garden Cities movement. Her position was one based on the ancient classical virtue of proportion, tempered and informed by the rising nineteenth- and twentieth-century concern for social justice. In a singularly well-chosen metaphor she asserted: "The towns are, in essence, big posters to attract first the investor in town-lots and second the capitalist manufacturer who will make town-lot values yet higher; but the expense of the advertisement seems out of proportion to the general wealth of the Province. All the costly paraphernalia of modern city life is certainly quite out of proportion to what production there actually is at present in city industries." She continued:

> Real Estate men are shocked at the idea of any change in the direction of municipal or provincial landlordship of all new town-sites, to be secured at agricultural value. "It would hinder Canadian development!" It certainly would hinder the recent artificially-fast growth of towns, but I have tried to show how detached this growth is from the general healthy development of the Province. Such a provision would hinder the ups of speculation, it would also be a much-needed brake on the downs; and in these days, when capital goes out to the ends of the earth, and to its most violently disturbed parts, it is hardly probably that any sound opportunity for industries would lie long unnoted for want of a chorus of professional boosters. Rather the great new Canada would still advance, but in different spirit, the old distinctive Canadian spirit of sober and well-considered adventure (pp. 121-22).

Unlike many less sensitive visitors from abroad, Mitchell felt that the benefit conferred by her year in Canada worked both ways: if she had advice to offer the rising generation of thoughtful Canadians on the management of their affairs, she was also grateful for having had an opportunity to watch a new society in the making. For Mitchell, Canada was producing a new-world version of an old-world model. The crucial difference, in her view, lay in the factor of time: time in its aspect of pace or speed, and time in the sense of historical process. "The cinema of life works monstrously fast out here," she remarked in reference to town life in the west (p.10). Moreover, the show was being continuously run all around her:

> One can watch the whole development of the Industrial Revolution and the Nineteenth Century displayed not in a series of years, but in a circuit of communities; one can pass from a newly-settled country township, forty miles from the railway, where nearly everything has to be home-made, through the successive stages of the prairie village, the railway divisional point, and the infant city with its great ambitions, on to the city of brick and stone, established but hardly secure, like Saskatoon, Regina, Edmonton, or Calgary; and so finally to great Winnipeg, throned triumphant between the New and the Old (p. 110).

Winnipeg, with its millionaires' residences on the Crescent, and its growing squalor in the North End — its wealth and power contrasted with its smoke and overcrowding — may not have been as "triumphant" as this passage suggests it was. Quoting from a paragraph in J. S. Woodworth's report on the activities of Winnipeg's All Peoples' Mission, Mitchell enumerated the proliferating health and social service agencies of the city and then commented, "The list is long; it has a terribly familiar sound" (p. 141). And she concluded:

> For the present it is clear that with all her good stock, and her vast spaces, and her advantage in starting to make her great cities after her mother Britain and her cousin America had gathered such painful experience, still Canada has not solved the problem set to the modern State, "To prevent the slum." And indeed, where everything moves fast, city conditions seem to degenerate with a horrifying speed, and with each year the task of mending becomes more difficult. It is clear to me in quite a new way, since I have seen the stages with my eyes, that our characteristic nineteenth-century civilization necessarily and definitely, in the best circumstances, with the best human materials, takes from some of her children what she loads so overwhelmingly upon others. In what makes a man, the homeless labourer of the cities is poorer than the loneliest and poorest pioneer on the prairie. There is far more happiness and far more health in the far-off prairie settlements that in the great rich cities; only, nobody believes it, and every little town is straining every nerve to be big (pp. 143-44).

Reading these words in 1981, one is tempted to remark, as Elizabeth Mitchell herself did in summing up her impressions of western life in 1914, "Plus ça change, plus c'est la même chose."

Department of English   SUSAN JACKEL
University of Alberta

Railway. At least I was not held captive by " the world of success and luxury," with the " soft and powerful influence," so accurately noted by Mr. Arnold Bennett as affecting more distinguished visitors to the American continent. I saw his " Woman of Wyoming's " parcel arriving, and being unpacked in the presence of a family hopping with excitement ; only she was a woman of Alberta, and her mail-order house was at Winnipeg. Also, I was in the West as a private person, not as a representative of any society or propaganda or business interest ; therefore I was allowed to look at things for myself and did not have everything shown to me. If I may borrow a metaphor from President Wilson and picture Canada as a noble tree with great branches and rich leafage conspicuous to all the world, then I was not placed where I could see the full proportions and outline, but I was down on the soil very near the roots, and from there I could peep up through the branches and perhaps see something of their connection with each other. It is a point of view that has both loss and gain.

About the second part of this book, I do not know enough to write it as it ought to be written. But there was a way in the West which a visitor soon picked up. If one wanted a thing done, and there was no proper person near to do it, one did it oneself as best one could ; and the result served for the time, till the proper person came to put it right.

As an outsider, probably I ought not to have ventured to speak so freely of Canadian institutions. But it is impossible for a Scot in Canada to feel like an outsider ; and it was never our Scottish custom to abstain from all criticism of our brothers and sisters. It is all in the family, and I do not think the family will misunderstand.

STIRLING,
    SCOTLAND.
December, 1914.

PART I

IMPRESSIONS

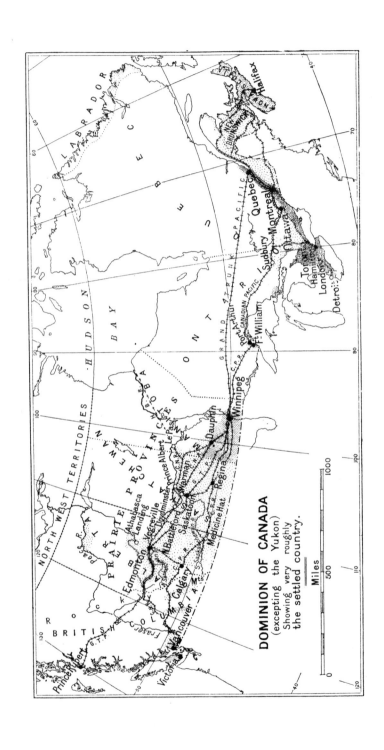

DOMINION OF CANADA
(excepting the Yukon)
Showing very roughly
the settled country.

Miles
0   500   1000

Not at all! The eye soon grows accustomed to little painted wooden houses and wide, straight streets of two-storeyed flat-roofed stores ; after a week one does not notice the unfinished look, the loose paper and the scraps of wood; one ceases to look for tall steeples and towers to break the sky-line, and begins to respect any tree over twelve feet high. After all, life is strangely the same. This funny flat chess-board of low buildings is really a town ; in fact it is the prairie town in its glory, on the verge of the change to the next stage, of brick and industries. " Business " dominates, modern Business with advertisement for a main feature. The chief citizens are substantial Business Men, deep in Real Estate, not dashing Rancheros or sun-browned Grain-Growers or anything in any way romantic. They do not ride wildly over the prairie, but sit in offices or travel on the train, busy " boosting the city " by all possible methods of " publicity." They are younger than their like in England, their ages ranging round thirty instead of round fifty, but they are of the unmistakable type of Anglo-American Business Men. They tend to grow bald, they dress very neatly, they drive in Ford motors to their suburban " cottages by the lake." Their wives, it is true, attend to their homes and children themselves and are glad if they can secure the help of one inexperienced girl or of a foreign

scrubbing-woman ; but these capable ladies finish
their work early and go out to each others' At
Homes in the afternoons in smart frocks and
feathers. There are picture palaces, magnificent
school buildings, telephones to shop with, hot-air
furnaces, electric light, water-supply laid on,
cement or wooden " side-walks " to keep the
smart frocks out of the mud or dust. There is a
" Social Rush " of teas and bridge parties and
dinners for the married ladies, and tennis and
dances and drives for the girls ; there are church
meetings and sales of work, and a baseball match
is not in essence very different from a football
match ; and the vast British Peace broods over
it all. There are no shots in the street, no quarrels
even, and what drinking there may be is not conspicuous on railway platforms or public places.
Propriety reigns on the whole more strictly than
at home, even a certain puritanism in some departments—*e.g.*, ministers of religion are definitely
expected not to drink wine, and are frowned on if
they smoke. History began here eight or nine
years ago, and the population is gathered from
the ends of the earth, yet the settled peace and
perfect security are far greater than in many
streets of our English and Scottish cities. Any
comparison with the early days of the Western
States is out of place.

This is the second impression, following on the

first strangeness to the eye. " Plus ça change, plus c'est la même chose."

Then other strangenesses appear. Go down the main street on Sunday evening after ten o'clock. It is full of Chinamen. Lose yourself in an outlying corner of the city, and ask the way. It is very likely a Galician settlement, and your only chance of getting an answer will be if you understand very bad German. The navvies at your front door digging the deep grave-like trenches (needed to keep water pipes from the frost) are Italians, perhaps with a broken-down Englishman of good connections at the end of the line. Little do his people realize that this is how the son of the house is " making his way in Canada." What has been the errand of that Mounted Policeman who comes riding down the street, so proud and soldierly ? Are these Indian braves whispering outside that store, in long great-coats, their ears protected by black handkerchiefs, their black hair in two long plaits ? Who is that unshaven besheepskinned ruffian on an ox waggon, with bright blue far-gazing eyes, and a face as dusky red as any Indian's ? Go to the hospital of the Sisters of Providence with a book or two and some flowers—the kindly French nuns are glad to welcome any visitor to their friendless patients. Here, in one ward, are a Londoner, a Frenchman from Paris, an old German (speak-

Also, even in the city, there are real differences
from old country or Eastern ways, besides the
superficial ones.   It is not true of any of the towns
or villages that " there are no social distinc-
tions " ; lines begin to be drawn in the tiniest
hamlet, and in a " city " like M—— (say, 7,000
inhabitants) society is quite exclusive, only the
line is a line of wealth and can be crossed ; but
what *is* true is that the differences between riches
and poverty are far less.   The richest families
have but one servant, and are lodged in brick
three-storeyed villas ; the husband works at his
business, the wife is busy in the house working
with her own hands.   On the other hand, even
in the depressed summer of 1913, there was in
M—— (N.B., a *small* city) hardly any poverty in
an English sense.   Workmen owned their own
houses ; shop assistants and typists and clerks,
on good wages, in fresh prairie air, with hope and
prospects, were browner and stronger-looking
than at home, and had an almost startling independence of manner.   To a discreet approach they
would respond kindly, but any suggestion of
lordliness would be put down at once.   This
approach to economic equality seems to me the
great charm of the prairie city ; it is delightful to
find a place where for the moment there is no
idleness on one hand and no hopeless ugly poverty
on the other, where every citizen feels he has a

chance, and all are immensely busy and therefore happy and healthy minded—seriously happy like busy children, not humorous like doubting, trifling seniors. However, the inhabitants of M—— would not all agree in this theory of its charm and absence of morbidity. Some of them thought all the world of it, not because it was a little bright, busy place, where nobody was very poor or very rich, but because it was going, they said, to be a great smoky city like Winnipeg, and some people in it were going to be very rich indeed.

Meantime, however, M—— is not like Winnipeg. Compared with ordinary city-dwellers, the 7,000 inhabitants are like trees in a well-thinned plantation, each counting individually, not indistinguishably crowded together. This explains the extraordinary sensation of busy complicated life that can be produced in these small places. In England 7,000 souls would make a small, unnoticeable town ; but in England an enormous mass of the population does not seem to count— the distinguished citizens are a very small percentage ; while here every man is a possible Mayor or Minister of State. Just as the buildings in the Western towns are scattered over a vast area, and make a tremendous show in proportion to their numbers, so a few people seem like a great many, because none are negligible. A place of 7,000 inhabitants on the prairie really seems equivalent to a bustling town of 70,000 in England, and one ceases to wonder at its being a " city." In its bustle and changefulness, and also in the vastness of the prairie district of which it is a centre, it *is* a city, and no stiff Britisher need laugh. After all, in the days of Lysander, great Sparta's citizenship was not great in numbers. Mere size is a modern fetish.

The stiff Britisher is certainly tempted to smile sometimes. Though business men put on such airs of solidity, the men and the business are after all but young, and have their ups and downs. If the Mayor of the City is well under thirty, and trusted Aldermen look about twenty-five, nothing can be quite as in the old world or Down East; the cinema of life works monstrously fast out here, and the figures come and go bewilderingly. Society regrets to hear that one acquaintance has disappeared, and that another is shovelling coal for an honest living; one household goes back to Chicago, another to London; and the new-comer who stays to see the May-sown annuals flourishing in the garden is far on the way to be an old inhabitant. It follows that people are friendly when they meet, for they may never meet again; they are kindly and willing to help any trouble they have time to see; but they are busy and forgetful. One goes and another comes, and out of sight is out of mind. The city must be boosted, the fortune must be made. " Canada is not the place for weaklings."

In the city, but scarcely citizens, are two special classes, the Chinese cooks and laundry-men, and the Galician labourers. The Chinese (all men and boys) know little English, and are always, apparently, at work; there are about a hundred in this little place, 1,000 miles from the Pacific. The Methodist Church tries to do something for them. The Galicians, though not racially separated like the Chinese, do not seem to mix quickly like the Scandinavians, Dutchmen, and Germans. " Galician " is a vague word, tinged with contempt, that lumps together Ruthenians, Roumanians, Slovenians, and South-Eastern Europeans generally, who come west in enormous numbers. Peasant people, dropped suddenly into this strange hurrying environment, they have their troubles. What is to be done with a handsome girl, sent up by the railwaymen from the station, who sits serenely hour by hour in your kitchen like a gipsy queen, but responds to no available language? Presumably she wants to go into service, but at her present stage she is not very easy to place. These people often establish themselves in dismal tumble-down little settlements two or three miles from town, where they are allowed temporarily to use building lots without buying them. Few know much about them;

they have no priests or leaders, and are cut off by difference of language and civilization. The Anglican Rector of M—— was much interested when a Ruthenian wedding party arrived at his door, and the spokesman explained that he seemed the most proper person to marry the couple, but that first they must confess. The confessions, like the wedding ceremony, had to be conducted through an interpreter—one hopes that 'neither conscience was burdened with very deadly sins. The " Galicians " may prove one of Western Canada's knottiest problems—there are so many of them—" but, meanwhile, they are convenient, they do the hardest work, why bother ? In Canada everyone finds his place." So speaks Optimism, and hurries off to open a handsome new Collegiate Institute and a new Post Office. There is so much to do, and so little time !

town (like others, I believe, in the West) is surrounded, not by smiling farms, but by a ring,
four or five miles wide, of unbroken barren
prairie. Speculation has divided it into town
lots, and sold it to distant investors ; meanwhile
it is useless. Even beyond this belt, there was an
enormous amount of uncultivated land, some
owned by the great companies (C.P.R. and Hudson's Bay) ; while here and there lay ugly
stretches of weeds, showing land that had been
" broken " and allowed to fall out of cultivation
again. After the first five miles the rich smooth
fields of the posters really did at times appear—
this part, one might be told, was taken up by
farmers from Down East—and again other fields,
with weeds rising above the wheat ears, or scantily
covered and full of gopher-holes. One saw little
Noah's-ark lumber houses, or picturesque untidy
hand-hewn log-huts. But the motors buzzed past
all the country doors to the Lake cottages, and
country residents did not appear in the city
parlours. There was no conspicuous in-and-out
class such as we have at home, with interests and
friends and influence both in town and country :
the vacant miles round the city might have been
a cholera cordon or a Roman frontier wall for
all the social intercourse that went on across it.

Observing these two sharply divided societies,
the British mind is startled to discover that here

business is socially at the top of the tree, and land-owning does not count at all. Rough country clothes carry no suggestion of ducal circles. The social convention is either that the country does not exist, or else that it is peopled by barbarians; and it is true that a homesteader who has driven twenty or forty miles in a heavy waggon over a hot dusty trail has a wildness in his look while he gets his groceries and inquires at the station for his machinery; in town he is not seen at his best. I found, in fact, that thousands of miles of journeying might bring the traveller very little nearer Canadian rural life. Happily I had connections which enabled me to cross the barrier. When that most hospitable house which had sheltered me in M—— was closed, I had arranged to go into the country. Friends in the town protested. I might have been proposing to start for the North Pole. " Going to stay on a farm ?—with Canadians ?—it will be very rough. You will not like it. Why should you go ? Do you know them ? " I was obstinate, and obstinacy was well rewarded, for the country was quite a new world, and there also I found the greatest interest and the kindest friends.

The start was characteristic. I was going to a farm twelve miles out, notoriously hard to find, but I had the most elaborate directions to guide me by a round-about way, supposed to be easier

to find than that by the usual trail,[1] which branched
a great deal. One particular only was forgotten,
that a certain road was in part made, but in part
only planned, and that it was not yet cut right
through to meet the main road ; and this proved
in the result to be troublesome. Starting gaily,
we soon left behind the fringes of the city, and
pushed eastwards along the great main road,
gloriously invaded by the many-coloured prairie
wild-rose, and bordered with splendid swathes
of Michaelmas daisy. Patches of wheat and the
all-embracing sunshine made a golden background. Eight miles or so out, " after Mr. ——'s
shack," we began to look for an opening on the
left, but seeing none, continued on the way till
we were sure we were miles past the right point.
" Be humble and ask the way," thinks the arm-
chair critic—but there was no one to ask, and no
human habitation visible but Mr. ——'s empty
shack. At last, moving slowly and doubtfully
along, we saw a binder and two men at work ;
one was a foreigner, one spoke English. " C——'s
farm ? "—he was not sure, but waved an arm

---

[1] A *Trail* is a natural track made by traffic, following the lie of
the land and running where people wish to go. As the country is
settled and enclosed, these are superseded by a gridiron of wide
made *Roads*, running perfectly straight north and south and east
and west. The districts I visited were mostly in a transition
stage, with some ways of each kind. A well-used Trail is fairly
smooth, the Roads are bumpy.

vaguely north-westward—" somewhere over there, several miles back." We embarked upon the open prairie to try a cross-country line, but clumps of small wood diverted us, and hay-trails wandered in an inextricable maze; we gave it up, and were relieved when the buggy bumped once more on to the main road.

Back we went, looking painstakingly for our opening on the right, but, as it did not exist, we went too far again, and struck off into the wrong road. Here also, no human habitation. The road ran through Company land, not yet open for settlement. Fireweed (our willow herb) grew high in the middle of the unused track, brushing the pony's flanks. Four miles of this were fatiguing and depressing. I felt we might indeed reach the North Pole, but nothing else. At last, a patch of cultivation, and wheatstacks! Where there are wheatstacks there must be a man. We shouted, we went up little hills, but the voices died on the air, no answer came. The sun was fast going down. My companion had given up belief in the existence of C—— and his farm. We were, of course, in no danger; we knew our way back to town, and the evening was warm and delightful; but, all the same, I began to realize with a new vividness the helplessness of the prairie solitude, the want of comfortable human contact. This was twelve miles from the city and the busy railway yards.

What about forty or fifty or a hundred miles
back ? and what about a winter's evening, with
the tracks covered by eight or ten inches of unbroken drifting snow ? We turned again, remem-
bering that we had thought we saw something
red half-a-mile off the track some distance past.
Again we tried a cross-country line, and again
thought the straight road the safer. There was
our red object, past a little bluff ; we plunged off
to it through the grass and scrub. Only a barn,
alas ! but just beyond it, a tiny box turning out
to be a one-roomed shack. Would the owner be
out in some far corner of his holding ? Would he
be an unintelligible Galician ? Would he know
C——'s farm ? He was at home, eating his
solitary supper ; he was a Canadian, and came
out to guide us to a commanding point. Now
C——'s farm was under a mile north-east, and if
we struck due across some prairie and some
ploughland, round some bushes and some little
mounds, keeping the sun behind us a little on the
left, we should find it—and so we found it, and
mightily enjoyed supper with the kind C——s.
We had gone about ten miles out of our way, we
had seen three men, and one of them was a foreigner.

One may travel to the Antipodes and hardly
change one's manner of life or subjects of thought,
but ten miles of prairie make a difference.[1]

[1] There was no " rural 'phone " in North Saskatchewan.

Battles might be lost or won in the Balkans,
" White Hopes " might rise or fail in the Ring,
but we should not know on the farms for a
week or more. The post came once a week to
the house chosen as post-office, and the neighbours dropped in from time to time, as it suited
them, to fetch their " mail." Newspapers and
letters came together ; but accounts of merely
passing events carried with them a fatal sense of
being past. So the sports column had lost its
grip, and country conversation flowed rather
with infinite variation round the neighbours, and
the crops, and politics local and general. Time
had recovered his old amplitude, and the
thousand hurrying modern voices died off in the
distance, " a confused noise without."

" . . . What wears out the life of mortal men ?
'Tis that from change to change their being rolls ;
'Tis that repeated shocks, again, again,
   Exhaust the energies of strongest souls
    And numb the elastic powers.
Till, having used our nerves with bliss and teen,
   And tired upon a thousand schemes our wit,
   To the just-pausing Genius we remit
Our worn-out lives . . ."

The Western country man has at least a large
monotony in which to mature.

III

I MADE my journey out of M—— about the end of August, and the prairie pictures in my mind are, all but one, framed in the gold of autumn. I never before enjoyed such continuously perfect weather as in these four months, September to December. First the harvest, then the freeze-up, then the slow tightening of the frost, never relaxed, but never unpleasant. On Christmas morning the temperature was below zero, but, still, in the delightful calm and dryness and sunshine, it did not seem to matter. It was during my last country visit of all, at the end of January, that the snow fell, dry and powdery, eight or nine inches of it, and the mercury dropped suddenly one night to 42° below (74° of frost), and stayed thereabouts. In a town house, with central heating and double windows and doors, I do not suppose one would have felt the cold seriously, but as it was, one felt as if there were a deadly beast just round the corner ready to spring at one's heart, and, indeed, that with a little extra bother a lazy heart might just strike work and stop beating altogether. The stoves were for the time the central things in life, and stuffiness entirely ceased to be a terror. Then in a few days the blessed " chinook " came over the Rockies—I was in Alberta then, not Saskatchewan—the temperature shot up to about freezing point, the snow dripped in the sun from the trees, doors and windows were flung open, we drew long breaths of relief and delight, and almost listened for the earliest pipe of birds— but the wise snow-birds knew quite well that this was not really the end, and all the others were far away, wintering in the South.

A country woman in a district I knew drove in to town that week with her milk, had a " frost-stroke " or " frost on the brain," and died a week later. The real Western cold, when it comes, is not necessarily very unpleasant or uncomfortable to feel, but it is deadly, it strikes at life ; and the better a man knows the prairie the fuller he is of almost old-maidish precaution. Also, the winter is desperately long. Early in November the freeze-up comes to still waters, the rivers hold out a little longer, according to their pace. The last green or brown leaf falls, the sap goes absolutely down, the spruces turn black (inconceivably more colourless than in winter at home), the prairie grass is grey. Colour does not return to the earth till well on in May, for long after the snow is gone the frost is deep in the soil, and nothing buds or blossoms. Only the skies are glorious day by day with sunrise and sunset.

This austere winter is the background of the country life. The short summer is a time of rush for the wheat-farmer with ploughing, " seeding," haying, summer-fallowing, harvest. The first frost comes, in North Saskatchewan, either in the middle of August or at the end, and that spoils the wheat unless it is absolutely ripe. Threshing comes at some point in " the fall," and is a great ceremony; the threshing outfit comes round with a gang of men, and the housewife has the busiest days in her whole year. The rest of the time from the freeze-up to the severe cold is the gay season on the prairie, the time for junketings and merry-makings.

In the districts I knew, wheat-farming was the general rule, especially in the newest settlements. Wheat requires only a few farm implements and a yoke of horses or oxen, hence it is popular with poor beginners, though mixed farming is probably less risky and more profitable—in some parts calves were booming like town-lots, and after church on Sunday farmers slapped their thighs and laughed to hear " the prices old man B—— got for his bunch Saturday." In wheat, just at first, the virgin land bears year after year, but in the third or fourth year the quality of the crop diminishes—this came as a painful surprise to many. Also a thorough ploughing is necessary every time to keep down the weeds ; where this had been neglected much land was almost as full of pigweed, fireweed, and wild roses as of wheat. In fact, the most successful method seemed to be summer-fallowing, keeping the land fallow one season and well ploughed and harrowed with a view to the next year's cropping.

The wheat-land was strangely silent. As one drove through it in the evenings one missed the comfortable sound of cows turning over in their pasture, or of sheep perpetually browsing by the way-side. The most characteristic sound was the cry of the coyote, the small grey-yellow prairie wolf, whose picture is in the books of Mr. Ernest Seton Thompson. The number and boldness of the coyotes was one reason given why sheep were not commonly kept (but in one place I saw sheep and coyotes apparently flourishing together) ; the other was an unpleasant spear-grass that worked itself into human beings' clothes and sheep's fleece, and caused sores. Once while I was paying a call at a certain farm-house north of M—— there was a commotion outside, and we all hurried to the door to see. A great drove of several hundred sheep was going north along the trail to a man who was going to be bold and experiment. We gazed after the strange beasts, and sniffed their sheepy smell; it was a tremendous event. Westwards in Alberta and its borders there is acknowledged sheep country; and sheep made a part of one of the most idyllic scenes I saw in the West. They were gathered, a great herd of them, on a grassy slope falling away to a little blue lake and a wide expanse of distant country, and their domestic familiar presence gave a kindly touch to the vast landscape. Above was a little grassy knoll, and a little wooden three-roomed house with a verandah nestling under it in shelter from the cruel north winds; and here lived, in peace and the fear of God, an old Englishman who had come from a rose-hung river villa on the Thames. His sons had married and left him alone, but he still preferred this life. Here he lived in all simplicity, doing his necessary work, baking his own excellent bread, busy and serene, bringing up his hired boy in sound religion and useful learning, helping the church in the neighbouring town, and receiving guests, when any reached his retreat, with a charming old-world courtesy.

Mr. R. stood outside the struggle of life; but most men come to the prairie to make their way. They come from Britain or Norway, or the Ukraine, "to take up a homestead" and to "make good" on it ; and perhaps some of them hardly realize, when they come, what " a homestead " is in North Saskatchewan—a quarter-square mile of grey-green prairie grass, with a tiny lake perhaps (a " slough," pronounced " slew ") and patches of small poplar wood. There may be no road, quite possibly no track, and no neighbours. Not so very far back from the railway the surveys are still being made by parties that go out in autumn from Prince Albert or North Battleford or Vermilion and disappear for months ; and where the survey has been made, and the checked map looks neat and finished in the landoffice, it is not always easy for any but the most experienced to mark the occasional corner-posts, and identify securely the actual bit of prairie answering to a given check on the map. Cases have been known of new-comers establishing themselves and ploughing and building on the wrong " quarter," and having a deal of trouble afterwards to get their position regularized. The homestead found, some kind of a house must be built, a certain amount of land must be " broken," and various needs must be provided for before the winter.

Where I went there were still a fair number of the log-buildings which mark the first stage. They were sometimes degraded to service as pig-houses or hen-houses, sometimes still in use as dwellings.

These are built of round peeled tree-stems, plastered with mud or some firmer mixture, and roofed with sod or hay or straw. A settler with a little more money, or no available wood, may bring out machine-sawn planks from town and make himself a " lumber" house, perhaps with two rooms at first ; and his wife will tell you, " If Johnny has time this winter, he's going to dig out some more of the cellar," or " he will make me another room" or " a verandah to keep the house cooler."

An unhandy man will build an untidy house (especially with logs), off the perpendicular, and tending to collapse ; but a log-house built by capable hands and efficiently plastered is far the most beautiful dwelling in the West, though it is not considered " the thing." The ends of the round beams supporting the roof make a natural ornament, and the individual arrangement and shape of the windows gives each house an expression of its own, like our old cottages ; such a house is also much warmer than the average lumber-house. The log interiors, unless all plastered and papered over, are tiresome for the housewife, because the mortar falls out of the chinks and the hay lining falls down from the roof; but their beauty is a delight. I shall not forget my first log-house. From outside I thought it was a hen-house or stable, not being yet accustomed to the style, but inside, how noble the vision was—the round brown beams dimly seen in the deep shadows of the pointed roof, the bright counterpane standing out with its full value in the absence of all fussy mixed unmeaning ornament, the splendid head of the strong old master of the house, the comeliness of his wife as she moved hospitably about the kitchen, half-seen through an open door, putting on the kettle and bringing out the tea-cups. " Are you dull out here in winter ? " " Oh no, we shut up early in the dark days, and my husband reads to me and I sew. We have read Dickens and Thackeray. We get through quite a lot." Another log-house was inhabited by a large family. It was long, with a pointed roof, and the length of it was divided off by curtains into women's room, men's room, and kitchen-and-living-room, into which the outer door led directly. Fixed partitions are difficult in prairie houses because with them one stove will not do for several rooms, and " a fire in one's bedroom " is not a mere luxury on the prairie in winter. In this house, as we gathered round the long board, and " put off desire of meat and drink," while the daughter of the house served and Mrs. S. dispensed the food, I could not help thinking of the Palace of Ithaca, with its somewhat similar arrangements. Ulysses is the perfect settler, painted once for all, with his

great thews and sinews and his many devices, his
equal powers for making a raft or a bed, or telling
a tale, or leading in council, or stiffening to
endure mischance. " That's the kind of man
Canada wants," and it is a kind she finds, too,
sometimes, or makes.

One vital fact is always to be remembered in
thinking of the Western country people as compared with country people at home. They or
their ancestors have not been the brothers and
sisters who stayed behind, but the brothers and
sisters who went out to face the unknown. They
have adventure and a fighting spirit in their
blood, and if they have less hustle than a townsman, the townsman need not assume that therefore they are " hayseeds " and dull fellows. Their
quiet is not lack of vigour. One becomes very
conscious of this. Also, they are young, while
the villages of older lands are full of fathers and
mothers whose children have gone away.

More than once I had the pleasure of knowing
men of leading in their districts. One was a
member of the Provincial Legislature ; another
acted as Secretary to the School Trustees (and, I
think, as most of the Board as well); another was
something very like a Presbyterian "ruling elder"
in a Church of England station. There was no
grandeur in the life of these Prairie Fathers, and
no haughtiness in their ways, though their neigh-

bours' esteem gratified them and still more their families. They were practical farmers first and all the time, and the member built a granary or milked a cow as well as anybody when he was not tackling more troublesome things. Some of these men had little book-learning—it was a vexation to them, but in the old days in the Ontario back-blocks learning was not easy to get. " I tell you," one said, " they talk of the hardships of the prairie, but it was a deal harder in West Ontario when I was a boy. The farm had just to be cut out of the forest, and there was only a single narrow track for a horse going out of the settlement at all. Every mortal thing from outside had to be brought on horseback." In such a place books were scarce and schooling difficult ; but for real education, for open mind, and careful judgment, and understanding of humanity, for plain dignity of manner and an honourable and laborious public spirit—to judge by its scholars, the forest must have been a good school. There are young men, too, of the same type, early married, fathers of families and responsible citizens, trusted by the townships with public functions ; and against all general maligners of the rising generation, I can testify that I have known on the prairie certain old-fashioned delightful families where the children (even the growing-up children) are neither forward nor rough nor

bit of garden in front, the berry-bushes, the
flowers in the window, the whitewashed clean
severity of the rooms—all were eloquent of the
older Scotland. The house was really of logs,
built up again by the owner and his sons after a
casual burning one afternoon a few years ago ;
I do not know how it was, but it managed to look
exactly as if framed of grey Scotch stone.

Sixty or seventy years had passed since certain
Highland emigrants had come to a Highland
village in Ontario. Children had been born and
grown up, Highlanders still. (Over the river,
I heard, had been a Lowland village, and not far
off an English one.) Then one young couple had
made the long pilgrimage into the Western wilder-
ness—thirty years ago or more, for my friends
were old-timers. They had come from Winnipeg
with their possessions in a waggon ; they had
something like typhoid fever by the way, and had
a poor time. They had settled and made a home;
and the third generation was playing round the
doors when, in '86, rebellion threatened among
the Indians. A friendly squaw gave warning,
" Better go to Barracks " (the R.N.W.M. Police
fort). The advice was taken, happily, and a few
hours later the house was burnt to the ground
and the Indians were exulting among the ruins.
Since then the West has changed. The railway
has come, and the new settlers, and even twenty

miles back from the line an old-timer may feel
almost crowded. But still the old squaw pays
occasional visits, and is honourably received.
She came when I was there, loaded with count-
less garments, a man's old coat on the top of
all. Her manners and gestures were elaborate,
her words few. She drifted in unannounced from
the distant reserve, where her people are settled
now ; towards evening she disappeared silently.

It was a surprise to find the ancient race so
strong as it still is in the Prince Albert and
Battleford districts. There are quite a number of
reserves—" John Smith's," " Thunder-child's,"
" Sweet-grass," and so on—which are secured by
the Canadian Government from white settlement.
There are Government teachers placed in some of
these reserves to try to teach the Indians to culti-
vate the land, but there was not much cultivation
so far visible—the work will require much patience
and devotion. Most characteristic were the
solitary bowed figures by the lake-shores silently
trapping musk-rat. Once I crossed a Cree Indian
reserve, and saw the little Roman Catholic
mission chapel with its bright vestments and
flowers, and its pews labelled " Abraham " and
" Moosomin " and " Grey Wolf " ; downstairs
was a little mission school, and as teacher-in-
charge a good Scot from Inverness who declared
he did not feel lonely at all. In other reserves

are Church of England missions and schools, *e.g.*, in " John Smith's," which lies in a beautiful valley near Prince Albert—the missionary here chanced to be another far-wandered Scot. Thunder-child, if I remember right, is as authoritative a Churchman as any old English squire, and objects to all Nonconformity, Catholic or Protestant, among his people.   The missionaries seemed to agree that the first effect of all the changes had been a quick decay of the Indian population, from consumption and other scourges ; but that now things were better and the remnant was like to live.   There appeared to be two quite distinct types in these reserves, one tall and good-looking, the other short and flat-faced.   In colour there really was not much to choose between an Indian of the reserves and a sun-painted prairie farmer ; and the Indian children in some of the schools, having lost their fine sunburn, were no darker than Italians.   In old-timer settlements, important citizens have often much Indian blood, and a full Indian has distinguished himself highly in a theological college at Saskatoon.   Individuals have proved their powers; the effort now is to help the communities to adapt themselves to the changed times without breaking up too soon.   I was present at a trial which illustrated the present ways of the reserves.   Canada does not believe in

amateur justice, and Law wore all her ancient
majesty. The case was one of shooting ; neither
the accused nor the injured nor any of the witnesses could speak English, so a half-breed interpreter had to be employed. There had been a
festivity—" a smoking "—on the reserve, and in
the evening a number of young men had been
amusing themselves outside of the hut of another
lad, the accused. The latter had become annoyed
" because they were knocking my door," so had
taken down his gun and shot vaguely into the
dark, bringing down two of the group. There
were many bamboozling cross-questions about
the wounds, but the witnesses said very little and
stuck to their points. " Was there blood ? "
" Um " (yes). " Where were you hit ? " A finger
pointed firmly to the complainer's middle. " Did
Thunderblanket say *why* ' he had shot 'em ' ? "
" Because they were knocking his door." Finally
Thunderblanket was admonished by the white-
haired authoritative Judge that he must not
hereafter be so hasty ; but, in consideration of
his youth and the number of people he was said
to support, he should not be sent to the Peni-
tentiary in that far land, Prince Albert—here a
grin of joy began to illumine the prisoner's
rather villainous features—he should stay with
the Police (R.N.W.M.P.) at the Barracks for four
months. A few minutes later I saw a most

cheerful prisoner driving off with his old friends the Police, relieved of a horrible fear.

This shooting was a domestic affair among the Indians. Among the white country settlers there are many shot-accidents (especially in the few days' season of moose-shooting in the forest) from the incredibly rough-and-ready methods of handling loaded guns—I have repeatedly seen men in hospital spoilt for life by pure carelessness. But as for criminal shooting or other crime, I never knew a securer corner of the earth than the North-Western prairie. Farmers' wives drive about alone in the dark across the solitudes without two thoughts. If you leave your house for a few hours, it is prairie etiquette to leave the door open. The passer-by may take food and light a fire, but he ought to extinguish the fire and chop more wood before he goes. Nothing else is taken. I heard one tale of horse-stealing, but not of a violent kind; there *was* certainly some "lawlessness" about close seasons for game. One hears that there is greater difficulty now in getting the right recruits for the Mounted Police, and there is occasional whispered scandal; but the general effect of the North-West is still that of a magnificently policed country. Long may the R.N.W.M.P. ride flourishing! Clearly it cannot be so easy now, in the midst of commerce and agriculture, to maintain the old combination of

the soldier's discipline and spirit and the frontiers-
man's dash ; but even now there may be plenty
of lonely adventure in a " Policeman's " career,
and there are still young men in the world out
for other things than dollars.

But mine is no gallant tale of camp and foray
and jingling bridle. Indians and Police and Old-
Timers are all alike survivals of an earlier age.
The modern country settler is a fighting man too,
but the weapons of his warfare are different, and
his enemy is not a bodily presence. He comes to
wrestle long and hard with Frost and Drought
and Solitude and Poverty. With many advantages over the men of the past, he has one enormous disadvantage, he does not belong in the
same sense to a strongly-marked united community fighting together. The day of the Highland or Lowland or English villages is past.
Western Canada is a melting-pot like the States,
of still more heterogeneous elements. A unity
will be made in the schools, one wonders exactly
what unity ; meantime, as the Northern proverb
says, " bare is back without brother behind it " ;
a Dane or a Galician or an American, dropped
down next you a year ago, may be a good
kind neighbour, and yet cannot be quite the
same as a man of your own dialect and religion
and ways, the son of a man who crossed the
" waste of seas " with your father, and who

used to work the next croft on the far-off "misty
island."

In certain parts, however, friends have settled
near each other, or at least a number of people
of more-or-less the same type. In a young settlement the first rounds of the great struggle may go
very merrily. There is hardly any money in the
community, the young bachelors " shack " in the
most primitive manner, but there are glorious
hopes, and it is all such fun. The harvest and
threshing over, the time comes for Socials of all
sorts, and above all for Dances on every occasion
and in any sort of space. The blizzard may
sweep past, the fierce frost may creak horribly
outside the warm log kitchen ; the country youth
will but grasp his partner the more firmly, and
dance on till daylight makes it possible to go
home safely. On a wild night, a wandering
" minister " lost his way in a hopeless solitude,
and had to give his ponies their heads ; they
brought him, a welcome guest, to the S.'s log-
house, where a gay party of twenty were dancing
the night through. A grandmother, in the light-
ness of her heart, will show her skill in the Highland Fling. Certain persons are famed as good
" callers-off " to keep the time for the dancers.
One settlement I knew—it was mainly English—
went utterly dance-mad one winter, and a hard-
worked housewife declared that her household

" chores " almost did themselves when she went through them to a dance-tune.

I remember very well my first country entertainment—a Home-makers' Tea. The house in which I stayed in town was one of the few which had links with the country, and its mistress was asked to address a Home-makers' Club Meeting. We drove ten miles on the north road, and dismounted at a curious isolated box of a building. It was a prairie school, and the company were gathering. Punctuality on the prairie is anywhere within an hour; there is nothing to set clocks by, and drives are long. On this occasion I noticed that the school-clock was half an hour fast, and we were nearly an hour and a half late by its time before things went ahead. There were fine faces among the country-women who assembled, strong mouths and straight eyes, and quiet foreheads, as of those who had looked Fate in the face and had not been cowed. They were full of hospitality and kindness, but who was I among these mothers of the Gracchi ? I felt myself a poor spinster from a smaller world, and I went and hid in a corner with the schoolmistress, who was a spinster too, and marvelled at the goodness of the babies, who attend all ceremonies in the West. After the address there was a splendid tea, with home-made cakes and ice-cream brought by the members, then there was business conducted in a

most business-like way by the president. There
was to be a Home-makers' Week at the University
of Saskatchewan (in Saskatoon).   Could any
members of this Club go ? They were to live in
College and have lectures and a great time.   A
delegation was arranged, and the meeting came
to an end, and I went away not knowing which to
admire most, the business gifts of the Canadian
farmer's wife, or the practicality of the University
of Saskatchewan.

Later, I became a friend of this club, and had
the privilege of addressing it myself ; and I heard
a great deal about the Home-makers.   The Clubs
answer to the Women's Institutes in Ontario and
the Country-women's Clubs in Alberta, and are
patronized by the University.[1] They meet once
a fortnight or once a month. They help shy and
lonely women, by making an easy way for them
to meet others ;   the addresses are usually on
some practical subject, like butter-making or
children's diet.   In the winter, I was present in
the same school-house one evening at the Home-
makers' and Graingrowers' combined Social.
There were songs and speeches and recitations
and competitions ; and there were very good
things to eat—pumpkin-pie was one—and there
was very nearly a dance at the end, but the idea
was started rather too late. The fathers seemed

[1] In Alberta I think the Minister for Agriculture takes charge.

to take charge of the babies this time, and it was the prettiest sight to see a magnificent young giant obliged to refuse the company a song because his two-year-old little girl had fallen asleep on his knee. The chairman was much commiserated on the temporary absence of his wife, and was presented, as some poor comfort, with all the food that was left to take home with him. Once more I saw the Roman Matrons in conclave. It was not in a bare prairie-school, but in a fine room in the city, on a great and significant occasion. 1913 was a hard year for the cities,[1] and for the first time in their short history they had leisure enough from humming business to think about the country; at the end of the year a Farmers' District Conference met for the first time in M——. The farmers' wives, including representatives of many clubs, met in another room, heard the latest views on Poultry-marketing, and discussed Prices and the Suffrage in a controlled but purposeful manner. Then they went on their way, and I saw them no more; but I was very proud later when in a certain district of Alberta a Country-women's Club was formed partly because I had talked so much about the Home-makers of Saskatchewan.

One word about the "roughness" of the country. The life is rough, in the sense that there

[1] See Part II, chap. v: Tight Money.

are few luxuries and only simple comforts in the
best-provided homes ; and what with the distances and the hard winter climate, in case of
sickness or accident or anything that breaks
routine, anyone *may* have to face terrible things
by himself or herself—life has the padding off.
But does the rough life make rough people ?
Doubtless I saw the pleasant side of everything,
because I was so exceedingly fortunate in the
homes which received me ; no doubt there are all
sorts on the prairie. I personally encountered
nothing but courtesy and kindness. I believe
some of the general theory of roughness is due
simply to want of acquaintance and some more
to surface appearances. The average prairie
man's very irregular habits of shaving may have
something to do with it. There are reasons for
this—the water is preposterously hard, and on a
prairie-farm all water and especially *hot* water is
a precious liquid ; even so there are some deter-
mined men who shave every day and are greatly
to be respected—the average character gives up
the effort. Let the finest gentleman in the world
go a few days unshaved, dress him in overalls,
and set him to shovel manure, or wrap him up in
sheepskin till only his nose is visible, and if he
speaks in monosyllables between his teeth it will
at least take time to detect his blue blood. Really
Canadian rural ways are extraordinarily neat

considering the great difficulties. The universal
overalls are an instance—nobody goes to dirty
work in woollen clothes that will not wash. For
some purposes some men wear the gay Indian
beaded buckskin coats, which are very service-
able as well as very beautiful. Canadians keep
their hands carefully; the inexperienced old-
country man or woman is apt to be careless and
soon suffers in winter. The typical Canadian
farm sitting-room has oilcloth on the floor, and
no heavy hangings or trimmings to catch dust
and dirt, so if a little straw, say, or mud, does by
accident get in, it can easily be swept out again—
but this is not allowed to cause carelessness, all
" clutter " is severely discouraged. On another
side of conduct, it is noticeable how more than
merciful the prairie man generally is to his beasts.
Whips are very often not carried ; I once touched
a slow old mare with a leaf to see what would
happen, and she all but bolted, she was so unused to such indignity. I heard of one man with
a reputation for cruelty, and it stood as a mark
against him for miles around.

At the sound of the word "prairie" picture
after picture comes back to my mind, beautiful or
comical or primitive, far too many to fix—a dark
farm-kitchen on a rainy morning and a literary
friend throned on a high chair talking philology
with the hired-man—a morning drive behind

two mettlesome young cart-horses, with the rime on the grass and an old grey coyote peeping carefully over a hillock—an autumn round-up on a horse-ranch, with the agitated herd sweeping round the corral while the foals were lassoed and branded—a great deal of dish-washing with very little water—high converse of " men, manners, climates, councils, governments "—passionate crusades against flies—a glorious empty golden valley, and a Pixie with golden hair like the poplars—a little potato-picking—a musk-rat flopping in and out of a half-frozen stream—and the line of railway lights across the still broad midnight prairie on the night I left Saskatchewan.

Since seeing Western Canada I can hazard a guess at the reason. I think the spoiled daughter of the millionaires inherits the position of a very different person, the pioneer woman, who earned it.· The burden of Empire-making most truly rests on the prairie woman, and she is often worn and old before her time ; she has little ease— but she has great honour, she is really a queen ruling in her domain. The words suggest cant and exaggeration, but there is none. Of all delightful things about the West perhaps the most delightful is that one escapes from all the modern strain and dislocation in the relations between men and women. There is no division of interest here, no idea of men losing what women gain. Far away from the railways and the factories, out among the primitive necessities, a woman needs a man's help, and a man needs a woman's. A woman alone is helpless as a pioneer, she simply has not the muscle required—but on the other hand the average man is very fairly unhappy " shacking." For a man in the West, marriage (in its outward consequences) does not mean what it does among the well-to-do at home, giving up comfortable bachelor lodgings for an elaborate expensive life of house-owning and smart little dinners and trimmings generally ; it! means leaving a ghastly loneliness for companionship and help, and squalor for decent comfort.

For a woman " the sphere of the home " does not
mean pouncing upon scratches on silver or
decorating the drawing-room with " masses of
flowers," but feeding and clothing and cheering
husband and children, and being kind to poor
bachelors round about who need kindness badly.
Woman is at her old task as the civilizer, not as
the over-civilizer. The problems of the independent woman-worker have not yet arisen.
There can be no economic competition between
men and women, no underselling by women, for
a girl cannot do the work of a hired man on a
farm ; and there can be no sweating of women,
for in the West, especially in the country, girls
are rare and command good wages—and a choice
of husbands.

The Western Peace does not really help us
much with our questions at home, where all the
conditions are so different, except in so far as it suggests that wealth takes away woman's most natural
dominion just as much as the extremer forms
of poverty ; but anyhow it is a cheering sight to
see, and may prevent one from forgetting certain
elements necessary in a right ideal. On the prairie
the woman is the true partner as well as the wife,
both as making the home and as helping with
useful details about the farm—poultry, butter,
etc. Sometimes she supplies useful book-learning,
having " taught school " before her marriage.

There is no question at all of inequality, the partners have their several departments, equally important, and the husband is the first to admit how much he owes to his wife, and to own that the burden falls on her heaviest. The absence of women neighbours, the impossibility of getting a hired girl to help in times of weakness, and the impossibility of affording doctors' visits are serious things for a woman, and this is where the pioneer suffers, no matter how kind and helpful the husband may be.

Canadian men in the West are usually very helpful, not at all " John Grumlies." They are always hewers of wood and drawers of water, and on a Sunday they may turn on to wash the dishes, giving their wives a change—they are clever at housework, having mostly had some experience as bachelors. The Old-Country husband has a bad reputation on the prairie (among the men), as leaving too much to his wife. One man occasioned quite a scandal by allowing his wife to help him harvesting (he was not strong) ; another gave offence by making no attempt to give his wife, who had been a woman of leisure, any better dwelling than a wretched sod hut. But, in any case, the man *has* to go out to his work, and the wife *has* to look after the babies and cook the food and bake the bread and do the washing and keep the house decent, though she may leave any egg-collecting or milking to the man at bad times. There is no one to help ; and so many a woman dies and many a baby dies, and some lose their health and their bloom, and many a wife is the cause of her husband's leaving the country and going to town. The provision of more hireable girls is one of the pressing problems of the prairie ; sometimes the wage is an impossibility, often the wage would be willingly paid, but girls simply cannot be had. From the employee's point of view the difficulty is partly the very hard work, partly the lack of reliable information. How is a girl to know how she will be treated in the remote spot to which she is asked to go, or even whether it is a safe and respectable place. The loneliness of the farms puts her for the time utterly at the mercy of her employers. Perhaps the Home-makers will add an Information Bureau to their other activities, and take some kind of collective responsibility for girls going out to a district. Something of the sort seems to be much needed.

Ordinarily, it is marvellous to see how the Canadian country housewife manages. She is the product of generations of pioneering, and difficulties have called out her powers. She is most able and competent, she applies her brains to housework, and also she has a tradition of how to do things best with simple apparatus. Thus the Canadian house is generally neater than that of the recent Old-Country immigrant, and at the same time the mistress is not so burdened and perpetually rushed. Labour and discomfort are avoided by, for instance, the simple suitable living-rooms I spoke of, the mosquito gauze over all the windows and doors to keep out all flies, the shed outside for a summer-kitchen in the months when the stove would make the house unbearably hot, the constant use of the important cellar. The prairie woman arranges the work and the house, wastes no steps, and puts through an extraordinary amount of work with no fuss or scrimmage ; and at the end, whatever her sufferings and labours, at any rate she is not a drudge, but a strong and generous personality—as I described the Home-makers—one in whom the heart of her husband can safely trust, and does trust. If the prairie women want anything that their husbands can get for them, they will not have to ask very long.

Generalizations are more rashly made and more likely to be wrong on this subject of " women " than perhaps on any other on earth. I should like to qualify every sentence in this chapter with a " generally " or " usually " or " as a rule," but the most patient reader might break down, and the qualifications must be taken for granted. In the more complicated society of the towns, the difficulty of analysis becomes still greater.

As in most things, so in the position of women, the small city stands at the point where two civilizations meet and overlap, the life of the prairie on the one hand, world-old, yet eternally young, and on the other the organization of society as we know it, on the nineteenth century pattern, a little *démodé* now, but still without a successor. As to the married women in these towns, most of what I have said about the prairie women is true, only not so much so. At the first beginning of the towns, the women practically *are* pioneer women, like their sisters farther out, and even a few years later, help being so scarce, they have still enough and sometimes more than enough to do of genuine importance. They are still capable managing excellent housewives. There is still not the smallest inclination to copy men's ways for smartness[1]—it is good enough to be a woman. Thus women do not smoke, and I found I was doing quite the wrong thing when I worked in a front garden one day with a wheelbarrow. In England any duchess may make herself as muddy as she chooses in her garden, but in the West that is a man's job, and to keep up my hostess's character I had to try to confine my improprieties to the secluded back-yard. I

---

[1] A totally different thing from the invasion of professions and trades and privileges for a livelihood or for an adequate sphere of action.

quite see the reason for this taboo, for the women have hard enough work with their sweeping and cooking, and after a business day a little digging is good for the men—but it was an interesting example of a natural custom hardening into a rigid social law, not fitted to the exceptional case of the lady who neither had very heavy house-work nor a man about the house to dig the garden for her.

Even among the married women, in a city say ten years old, there are marked differences from the prairie situation. Half of their work no longer deals with the primary necessities—the labour saved by electric light and water laid on is spent on larger and more elaborate houses and on " social duties." Women wear themselves out now in polishing wood and silver and in keeping smart drawing-rooms clean—and thus house-keeping is still burdensome, but it is no longer so vitally necessary or so personally interesting—it has lost the splendour and reality of a fight for life. As wealth increases, this kind of work may be left to servants, but in the little city that is not altogether possible, it is only an ambition ; a delicate wife may occasionally cut the knot by taking her family to live in a boarding-house. Everywhere in Canada servants are expensive and difficult to deal with, and the boarding-house solution is tempting, as it has been in the States

—and where is woman's sphere then ? In another way also the richer city wife has lost what the prairie wife had. She does not share with her husband at all in his work. He goes to his office and is lost in the golden clouds of finance—and following American and English precedent, unlike the Frenchwoman, she stands quite outside. She has narrower and more purely "feminine" interests than the prairie woman (*e.g.*, clothes, bread-machines, and hired-girls), and she has far less reality in her life and character—but she has an active mind and the beginnings of leisure, and in time to come, if things must go on as they are doing, she will probably realize a want, and set about something like the American woman's curious detached pursuit of culture and pleasure and Causes to satisfy the soul.

The City-girl in the West already corresponds nearly, I should guess, to one American type. The hard-worked mother lets her daughter take her pleasure while she can, and makes little claim on her. There is no governess or boarding-school to take the trouble of discipline, and circumstances do not provide so much as on the prairie. Very often the girl has a profession or occupation (as teacher, stenographer, or store-clerk), but the salaries and hours of women's work in the West are comparatively easy, and always she can have a real good time in her leisure. She has it, and

looks after herself most efficiently. Then marriage
comes, the girl settles down to the hard work of
life, and proves triumphantly that she could cook
quite well all along.

·The grace of girlhood, as old-fashioned people
admire it, is rare in the West, at least in the towns.
I have seen it in a prairie farm, against a background of stern simplicity, and I have seen it
flowering exquisitely in the family which one of
the finest of Canadian ladies brought up among
the Indians of Hudson's Bay. I have seen it in
hospital blessing a whole ward. But it is rarer
than at home—and I have a violent insular
prejudice against all girls (and boys too) who chew
gum.

I thought the position of women generally in
the West was illustrated by the following fact. I
am told by good authorities that the habitual
language of these parts is exceedingly lurid ; but
I travelled endlessly in Pullmans and locals and
mixed trains of the most rustic description, I
waited on railway platforms, I passed through
hotel bars, I dined at small eating-houses, I was
in and out of a considerable variety of places in
town and country, and never a word of bad
language came to my ears, except from one little
boy who hardly knew what he was saying. The
reason cannot be simply deafness or absent-
mindedness in me, for I could not say the same

British exasperation, and has less of the " women against men " element. But the most interesting suffragists are the prairie women. They have good minds, and they are accustomed to be serious, and they do think about these things, and so there is a very noticeable movement on the prairie, quite free from any exasperation at all, and quite likely, I think, to succeed soon, so far as the Legislatures of the prairie provinces are concerned. As in New Zealand and the Western States, the farmers do not see any particular reason why their wives should not have the vote. The opposition will come perhaps from the financial interests in the towns for fear of " socialistic legislation," and almost certainly from the liquor trade. The special trouble which has turned the prairie women's minds to politics is connected with the land. The woman so obviously shares with her husband in making the "improved farm " out of the 160 acres of original prairie that it is felt to be an injustice that this product of their joint labour becomes the sole property of the man, and that he *can*, if he chooses, sell it and break up the home without his wife's consent. Cases where this has been done have raised a great deal of feeling, among men as well as women, and a Bill was actually introduced lately into the Saskatchewan Legislature making the wife's signature as well as the husband's necessary for the validity of any deed, whether of mortgage or sale, affecting the farm.

Any study of Western women's life would be seriously incomplete if it did not touch on the Servant Problem. In the country it is exceedingly difficult to get a girl; in the towns and smaller cities it is possible, but there are inconveniences. A certain couple of nice English maids arrived at M—— and said they were housemaids. They were greatly taken aback when they found that not even the smartest woman in town had two servants. The " girl " or " help " has to be prepared to try anything, and the mistress generally has to do the skilled work herself. A Galician or other " foreigner " or a little girl of thirteen or fourteen has drawbacks of one kind ; a competent " help," Canadian or British, besides being costly, will usually expect to have meals with the family and to share their life. This might be pleasant enough, if it were conventionally correct, with some old retainers at home, but with a constantly shifting succession of strangers it is genuinely uncomfortable, it prevents all ease of talk. The " help " is often free after three o'clock to go her own way (any later service being done of grace by special arrangement) ; but this is not unreasonable, as she works most energetically from an early hour.

Some rule of the kind may have to be made before long in England.

The lack of service has various results in social life in the towns. Teas are commoner as entertainments than dinners ; and this accentuates the social separation of the women and the men, so marked in comparison with either England or the prairie. People do not often go to stay in each other's houses except from necessity or with near friends. Visitors, when they *are* received, lend a hand with the work, and consequently a Western visit is a much more intimate thing than at home ; one makes acquaintance much quicker in the kitchen over a dish-tub or a cake-tin than sitting on a proper chair in a drawing-room with folded hands wondering what to say next.

Having no servants at all may be exceedingly pleasant. The town-houses are compact and well-arranged and full of labour-saving devices ; the furniture has few knobs and crannies ; and a woman in good health with an average family seems to find little to grumble at. Two women living together can have good meals and well-dusted rooms and yet get through their work early and have large leisure for hospitality and outside occupations. One's house is one's very own, and there is no one to look glum if a party of hungry travellers do turn up towards evening wanting food and lodging. The whole basis of life cannot be suddenly upset by Jemima's leaving without notice. The great thing is to decide what is most necessary, and concentrate on that. The real proud Canadian housewife does everything at home, but probably any woman unaccustomed to manual labour will be wise to spare herself where she can, to let some of the washing go out, and to have some one in from time to time for heavy scrubbing. It costs money, but it makes a tremendous difference to the housewife's health and spirits ; if she is spared this heaviest work and if she is willing to learn Canadian ways, an Old-Country lady may come through the ordeal of life in a prairie town not discreditably, and may even prefer it in time to the lap of luxury. But the housework cannot be shirked on any plea ; a saint or a princess with a messy house would have little position or following among Canadian women.

Miss Sykes has dealt in her excellent book, *A Home-Help in Canada*, with the question of openings for English women of education, and I only wish to add a few notes to what she says. Girls were still wanted, even in the bad times since 1913, though so many men were unemployed; but working-girls are the easiest to fit in. It remains to be seen how the War will affect women's employment out there ; but certainly no educated girl should go alone to the West without money to keep her for a few months or to buy her ticket home. As Miss Sykes says, there is no room at all for anyone wishing " to do light work," and Canada is a country where the feeble and ·inefficient find very little mercy. On one point in her account of " home-helping " I have a criticism to make : I think usually a home-help on the prairie has more amusement than Miss Sykes could have, staying as she did only a fortnight in each place, and at the busy season. But I quite agree with her that this is not a position for educated women, except in the houses of friends.

In teaching there was an opening for adaptable girls able to look after themselves and willing to take a short Normal Course for the Canadian qualification. I have heard a Deputy Minister of Education mourning over his lists. " Year by year we rush students through the Normal Colleges, we issue special permits by the dozen and the hundred, and still we are just where we were. Where do our teachers go ? They seem to disappear into the sandy soil! " The Minister had his suspicions as to the cause of the leakage, but it was not a cause he could remove. The salary-scale is fairly good, even considering the high cost of living, and women teachers seem to have more leisure and a far better social position than at home ; but there are at present practically

no " plums," as all the highest posts are held by
men. Most teachers have to serve at least a year
in a prairie school before reaching a High School
post. " Stenographers " (typists with shorthand)
were in demand, but I am not certain that this is
still true. There were numbers of nurses out of
employment towards the end of 1913, not that
there was not need for more nursing, but there
was no money to pay for it.

Thus the professional openings are very few,
and yet women are greatly needed. The young
woman is, of course, both the most needed and
the most difficult to arrange for, but there are
other curious gaps. In the youthful towns old
ladies are exceedingly rare and correspondingly
valued ; on any social occasion the white hair of
some visiting mother will prove the strongest
attraction, for amidst a certain inevitable harsh-
ness and crudity the memories and kindliness of
age are very precious. There are perhaps more
old people in the country, but even there the
grandmothers have the worship which sometimes
goes in England to the grandsons. As nearly all
the women are young and fully occupied with
young families, it follows that there is a lack of
women of leisure for the very necessary odd jobs.
Who is to look after the girls coming to town, to
spend trouble and time in getting them suitable
places, to help the foreigners to learn English, to

visit the hospital, to help a delicate mother with
bustling children, to sit on school-boards, to
organize the leisured girls, where there are any,
to do some kind and useful work ? One constantly
sees at home a pair of sisters or friends with a
modest independent income, settling down with
a touch of regret to grow old quietly in a town
where there are dozens or hundreds like them.
Many are capable women who never had their
opportunity, and some chafe inwardly as they
look down the narrowing vista ahead. If any two
sisters of spirit would simply go with a stout heart
and settle in any prairie town (outside of the large
cities) they would be busy enough and important
enough before a year was out, far too busy to
think about growing old for another twenty years.
There is a handsome roomy niche waiting in the
West for the Professional Maiden Aunt as well as
for the grandmother. As to the assured income
necessary, there are fewer " appearances " to be
kept up out there, but prices are far higher. An
income which in England has to be spent mostly
on necessaries would not in the West provide a
living at all.

One thing I think more girls from comfortable
homes might do, and that is go out to make homes
for their brothers. Life out West may be rather
a terrible thing for a young wife, but for a girl in
good health with her own familiar brother, it is

no more than an adventure which will bring out what is in her. The brother has a bad time by himself and is diffident about asking his sister to forsake her comforts for his sake ; but women are not really so wedded to luxuries as they are supposed to be, they are all Lady Catherines who " love to be useful," and few regret coming out in this way. Housework, even hard and monotonous housework, is so visibly different according as you are doing it as a hireling for people you do not care about, or zealously and honourably in your own house for your own people. Only let no girl, sister or sweetheart, idealize the prairie, or lay fine schemes that she will do this and she will not do that. She will have to do as things will do with her, and far the best training would be six months as a general servant either in England or Canada. Then she will be prepared for what is hard in the life, and will enjoy the more the many parts of it that are delightful.

VI

ONE may wholly disapprove of extravagance, and
yet admire the chief form it takes in Saskatchewan. This province plunges in education and
educational buildings in the wildest and noblest
way ; and the towered proud palaces that dominate the cities are schools. I never saw anything
like this proportion of expenditure in any other
country or in any other province of Canada that
I have visited. It almost suggests the concentration of the early Middle Ages, when the great
Cathedrals first soared heavenwards from the
little huddled towns. There may be mixed
motives, a contractor's interest here, a touch of
advertisement there—so there probably were
with the Cathedrals—but still these great schools
and the wonderful University stand for an aspira-
tion neither selfish nor material. " Their children
shall see it." The schools are a standing challenge
to the meaner spirit that declares " I'll make my
pile and get out down to the Coast."

Public Schools[1] and High Schools in the city, the great University at Saskatoon, the Normal Schools for teachers and the tiny schools on the prairie are all alike public institutions. There are no universities founded by private individuals, as sometimes in the States, and there are no denominational universities as there were down East. There are theological colleges affiliated to the University, one for Church of England students, in connection with an English Society,[2] another belonging to the Presbyterian Church of Canada. There may be others already existing or planned. As to schools, the Roman Catholics have in the towns separate schools[3] and school boards. Many parents dislike sending their children, girls especially, to the public schools, and Old-Country people often send their girls home or to some boarding-school in Toronto or elsewhere in the East. In the West itself, there

[1] Equivalent to our elementary schools, but attended by rich children as well as poor.

[2] The Colonial and Continental Church Society.

[3] The separate schools are supported by grants from the provincial government, and taxes levied upon separate school supporters. They provide their own buildings, and the board members are elected by the Separate School supporters.

The Public Schools may be opened with the recitation of the Lord's Prayer, and the half-hour previous to the school closing may be given to religious instruction as arranged for by the different Boards. Any child can be withdrawn from the religious instruction by the parents or guardians if they so desire.

are some good convent schools, and there is now an excellent boarding-school for girls at Prince Albert under Church of England control.

Education is compulsory—here Saskatchewan differs from Manitoba—and far out into the wilds the school follows the settler. The neat little lumber school-houses are characteristic features of the prairie landscape, standing bare and solitary, perhaps without another building in sight. I visited several of these little schools, one where nine out of the dozen pupils answered to one surname. There was a new teacher, and when she asked for names, she thought the children were up to some mischief; but they were the children of two brothers, and the school was practically a family party. The prairie teacher has not an easy task. She is generally a young girl, and in her single classroom she has to manage small children and great big boys, some well trained at home and some the merest young barbarians. In many districts there are foreign children who need special attention yet cannot receive much from lack of time. The children have no change of teacher to stimulate them nor any neighbouring school to rival. On the other hand, they rather like going to school, as it makes a change and an interest, and they are responsive to anything like a story. For technique, for skill in keeping five grades going at the same time and having eyes in the back of their heads, I greatly admired the teachers I saw. Some were extraordinarily good in keeping up interest. The reading-books seemed to me rather poor, especially in their verse, which was generally weak and uninspiring ; but there were good small libraries in some of the schools and some of the teachers introduced the children to the books. I have seen a prairie child devouring *The Child's Garden of Verses*, and again hiding in secluded corners of her home to gallop through *The Pilgrim's Progress*. One saw clearly here what one might suspect, that children are just as willing as ever to read books that are worth while if they do not get hold of " tosh " first. Rubbishy books and the ordinary cinema show call for no effort, and the power of making this particular effort is soon lost. Town teachers gave a dismal account of how rarely anyone read a real book through, and the libraries of one or two town schools I saw did not compare particularly well with the prairie libraries. There were certainly plenty of people in the country, young and old, perfectly willing to read a real book through, once fairly started. Excitements were not so common that any interest could be missed. I believe the very hardness and solitude of the prairie give Saskatchewan an opportunity for building up a real sound culture, neither fanciful nor fashionable nor bookwormish ; and towards this end, I wish something could be done about the " Readers."

Drill was not a regular subject in the Saskatchewan schools, and I saw a regrettable number of round backs ; but I think something is now being done to change this.

To return to the teacher, she is the belle of the prairie balls, the leading unmarried lady of her settlement. Often she plays her part in pretty comedies of courtship and disappears, as the Minister said, "into the sandy soil." Then her successor comes, as young and inexperienced as she was. Thus the average teaching may be bright and efficient and modern, but there can be no mature view of things or manly philosophy such as some of the old dominies of Scotland used to provide. There were dominies in Ontario too, I hear, not so long ago, and some of the men of to-day look back to the teaching of the village school as the inspiration of all their doings. Perhaps in one way the young school-mistress hastens the drift to the towns, though in another she undoubtedly adds attraction to country life. She is at an age when the gaieties of town almost necessarily seem the ideal, and young rustics are as quick as other children at catching an impression ; there might be uses for some crusty old fellow to whom a great city should seem a mere scarlet Babylon and a sink for the offscourings of the earth. However, few men are found to offer for these posts, and the bachelor payers of school-rate are inclined to pass over those who do, and to wear the colours of the " school marm," saying that, since they have no children to educate, in justice they ought to get *something* appreciable for their money.

But even outside of her classroom, the school-marm's life is not to be too rosily painted. I was in one district when a new teacher came, and the poor girl thought she would end by having to sleep upon the open prairie. There is no teacher's house, and in this case the farm nearest the school housed the teacher for a night or two, but could not keep her permanently. None of the busy women of the settlement really wanted another member to her family. There was no room, and it meant extra cooking, and threshing-time was coming near, and so on. A farm two or three miles from school offered a room and a horse on which the teacher could ride daily—but this was a town young lady with no skill in horses. Finally this individual problem was solved ; but one could see how very unpleasantly a teacher might be situated among foreigners with ways not too particular, or where few of the settlers were married. It is most difficult to get accurate information beforehand of anything on the prairie, except where the travelling clergy can help.

The prairie teacher is not troubled by too much inspection or interference from superior authorities who are very busy and very far away ; and the local school-boards are usually glad to have got a teacher, and willing to leave everything to her ; but if the local people should take a dislike to her, she will just have to go (I think a month is the notice required). Generally she has freedom and isolation, and a girl who likes responsibility will enjoy the work, and one who likes to be guided and protected will detest it.

There is talk now of " consolidating " the schools in some districts, *i.e.*, having larger schools at greater distances, and sending out vehicles of some sort to gather the children. This would prevent the isolation of the teacher, and it would make possible more specialized teaching and larger classes with more stimulus to work. I think the teaching profession as a whole is in favour of the change. On the other hand, it would rob the districts of their centre, for only in the school-house can everybody meet ; this useful room accommodates grain-growers and home-makers, political meetings and church services, and may come to be used in future[1] more than it is now. As centres are *the* need of the prairie life,

[1] *Cf.* President Woodrow Wilson, *The New Freedom*, chap. v, " The Parliament of the People," in the similar case of the country school-house in the States.

this objection is grave. Also the long drives about scattered settlements might, in this climate of extremes, be an undesirable preparation for school ; the better teaching might be neutralized by the weariness of the child. The question is very difficult.

I visited a number of the public schools in the cities and everywhere was amazed at what I saw, the great spacious sunny classrooms, with their comfortably fitted desks and their yards and yards of blackboard, the wide bright corridors, the flowers in the window-boxes, the beauty and permanence of the buildings. Boys and girls sit together in class but have their separate dressing-rooms off the classroom, and march out of school separately to the sound of music. It is co-education, but limited. I was asked to speak to some of the classes, and once was brought to realize sharply the difficulties of history teaching in the West. I came from Stirling, the year was 1914, one subject seemed obvious—the Battle by the Bannock Burn in 1314. I began to say something about the Castle which was to be given up on Midsummer Day six hundred years ago, if the English King did not come to save it ; but I soon saw my audience looking blank. Did they know what " a castle " was ? No! I had to say it was a place where soldiers were, something like the Mounted Police Barracks, and then to draw a picture on the blackboard of Stirling Rock and Castle and the hills on this side and that, and the windings of the Forth.   Further south, on the bald prairie, I suppose it would have been necessary to explain " a hill " too.

Amidst much admiration for the Saskatchewan public schools, one doubt creeps in. Is the building perhaps over-emphasized in comparison with the teacher, who makes the school after all ? For one thing, classes are too large, though probably not larger than in elementary schools at home. Then everywhere there are these young teachers, mostly girls, while even head-masters are not far into the thirties. Many men start life " teaching school," but turn off into law or business as offering greater attractions. There is a difficulty coming if few men remain in the profession, and at the same time the higher posts are in practice closed to women, that is to the great majority of the teachers. The women are discouraged from professional ambition, and the field of selection for headships is not wide enough. The great schoolmasters who have influenced England so strongly have been selected members from a host of keen and able men devoting themselves for life to the profession of teaching; and it is possible that the comparative lack of such teachers may be the cause of a certain thinness of thought and absence of strong moving ideas sometimes to be noted in great new countries. Canada has such a giant's task before her that she will need great ideas if ever a nation did.

It is everywhere the special temptation of business men in education to believe that a school or college is first and foremost a building; but at least at the head of educational affairs in Saskatchewan there are men perfectly well aware of this danger. President Murray of the Provincial University at Saskatoon knows that men not walls make a city, and the body of stone and mortar in his University will clothe and not eclipse the soul. I saw him rise once at a great ceremonial opening of a Collegiate. There had been speeches and speeches on the glories of the city and of the building, statistics and prophecies and all manner of magnificence. Dr. Murray lifted his grey scholarly head slowly, and smiled kindly on us all. All that was right in its way, but there was something else. "A school is not a building, and it isn't a school-board, it isn't even only the teachers. I want to speak to the boys and girls." And he did speak to them, very quietly and simply, for a very few minutes, and gave them something they would remember.

President Murray is one of the distinguished sons of Pictou County, Nova Scotia, where College Presidents and other good public servants have been " raised," it seems, by the dozen. He may

have no hustle in his manner, he may have a
quiet professorial air, but his conceptions and
accomplishments do not lack daring ; the University of Saskatchewan is the most startling
thing I saw in the West. For, if there is one pre-
eminent character in those Western cities, it is
the note of change, of rapid and amazing and
unpredictable change. Towns rise like vapour
from a river—one feels they might vanish as
quickly. A great iron-framed brick-faced business block is run up in no time, but it is a tran-
sitory thing, one feels it is not made to last. A
wooden house may come to meet you down the
street, and you will rub your eyes the first time,
but the third time you will scarcely look. The
very trees are all young, and whisper of trans-
plantation, not of immemorial roots ; and men
are here to-day and gone to-morrow, back to
Winnipeg or Chicago or down to the coast. One
receives this impression as sharply in the streets
of Saskatoon as anywhere ; one crosses the iron
bridge over the river and climbs the long hill of
Nutana through brick and timber villas, taber-
nacles for a shifting people to rest in; and then
one emerges on the bare prairie and sees the University. It is built of granite, solid granite
boulders from the Saskatchewan. It is not bare
or plain or primitive in itself, though it badly
needs the trees which have still to be planted, it

scholars come back, I heard, "with a terrible Oxford manner," but their friends hope this will rub off in time and yet something special be left.

Both Oxford influence and the classics might seem out of place in the youngest of Provinces, but perhaps they are really very much in their right place. For Platonist Oxford has never been satisfied with the ideal of mere abstract study or of an art and culture for an exclusive coterie. She has never been able to keep her thoughts long off the politics of church and state. How could she, while believing with one of her honoured sons "that the unity of human nature in its diverse activities is so intimate and pervasive that no influence can affect any one of them alone and that no one of them can operate or change without transmitting its influence to the rest."[1] Oxford has kept the magnificent aim of embracing in her studies the whole of human life ; and out West there is life enough, young and vigorous, and plastic. Of memorable Oxford men, Ruskin, I fear, would have loathed Saskatchewan, but William Morris would certainly have loved the mighty men of the prairie, and the homes that they build with their hands ; and so great and so practical a man might even have got a hearing in the centres, and fashioned a city after his imaginings—a little city, perhaps, but what would that

[1] Professor A. C. Bradley, epilogue to *Oxford Lectures on Poetry*.

matter if it were sufficiently glorious ? Morris would have recognized the antique outline of the prairie life, and the brotherhood of the true prairie men to the kingly farmers of early Rome ; he would have seen the daughter of Penelope and Nausicaa in the prairie housewife. This way of looking at things is not the prevalent Western one, and yet it may not be merely fantastic.

Beyond the Arts building with its lecture-rooms, as one tacks across the windy Campus, one catches sight of strange unacademic edifices. Here is a gigantic barn, and a great shed for farm machinery, for Agriculture is the characteristic faculty of the University of Saskatchewan and the Dean of that faculty one of its chief men. The farmers' sons come to college for their technical training, and in games and daily life they are thrown together with the Arts men, and both should gain something. This faculty is the one that interests itself in the life of the prairie women.

The Agricultural Colleges of Canada are splendid, and seem to leave nothing undone that can be done in this way to encourage farming ; only it is said that their graduates too often do not return to actual practical farming. I visited the famous mother college at Guelph in Ontario, and admired the glorious situation and the fine buildings and equipment. I saw specially the women's buildings for Domestic Science training. These are in charge of two most charming ladies, and I thought how wise an English girl would be to take a " home-making " course here before venturing on the prairie—but, unfortunately, the buildings will not hold the applicants, and Ontario farmers' daughters have the preference. Some Old Country society might perhaps make a deal with Guelph, and secure that a certain number of places should be reserved for Old-Country girls. At Ste Anne, near Montreal, an interesting experiment has been tried, originated I think by Dr. James Robertson, the well-known Canadian educationalist. Education often spoils the young for rural life—well then, said Dr. Robertson, let the teachers of our Province be trained in agricultural surroundings, let those who come from the country never taste the dangerous delights of town. So Ste Anne is primarily an agricultural institution with experimental farms, etc., but a provincial training-college for teachers generally is placed there, to be in an agricultural " atmosphere." In Alberta there is another effort to prevent town " infection "—for, surprising as the fact is, town attraction has really reached the point of disease in the Canadian social body. Alberta had, last year, no Agricultural Department at the University, but it had three Agricultural Schools, and these were planted out in prairie districts so that a young man might not have to come to Edmonton and be tempted to forget " all his toil and all his father's house." These are not colleges, they are for younger lads, still continuing their general education. They are, as it were, High Schools with an agricultural intention, and are very much needed in face of the strong urban bias of the ordinary High School.[1] Simple carpentering and smithy-work are taught as well as ordinary farm work—for these are settlers' institutions. They are closed for a six-months' vacation in summer, so that the boys may go out and earn as hired men. The school I knew was in charge of an enthusiast, and ought to do good work, but as it was only opened in autumn 1913, one cannot speak yet of results. The University of Alberta (at Edmonton) intended to organize an Agricultural Department shortly for more advanced work.

I must say a word in this connection of the Dominion Government Experimental Farms. There are several of these, but the one with which I had dealings was that at Indian Head near Regina, the oldest one, I think, in the West. I wondered what trees and flowering shrubs it was possible to grow in the severe climate, and wrote to the Indian Head farm explaining that I was neither a homesteader nor a tax-payer nor even

[1] *Cf.* Part II, chap. i.

VII

CHURCHES AND CHARITIES

ALICE Through the Looking-Glass was not more
confused than were some good Anglican church-
goers on first arriving in M—— from England.
Everything seems turned the other way round in
those parts. Matins are attended by a faithful
few, at evensong churches are crowded. Young
men may be seen going to church by themselves,
mistresses of houses incline to stay at home.
Church collections have to maintain church and
"rectory" and "rector's"[1] salary, the "duplex
envelope system" prevails, the English church
is no finer than the Presbyterian or Methodist
churches, and the "English minister" sits on the
City Ministerial Association with other "ministers." A member of the congregational vestry
may find himself urged to attend Synod as a
delegate, and he will find the Bishop associated
with an elected Executive; while a good sup-
porter of missions will not find seven or eight

[1] The title "rector" is given when the congregation is self-
supporting and requires no help from the central diocesan funds.

different societies to choose from, but one
" Missionary Society of the Church of England in
Canada," with its " Women's Auxiliary," embracing Home and Foreign Missions alike. It is
all " very Canadian " as seen from the English
side. But there is another point of view.

One has always to remember that the West is
not fully " Canadian " at present, it is Canadian-
American-British-Foreign. English people come
to a Western town, and note peculiar "Canadian"
habits, but the stray Torontonian writhes with
fury as he listens, since in his view the whole
place contains only three or four truly respectable
Canadians. In the medley, each of the large
denominations seems to have a racial or national
tinge, not always exactly what one would expect.

Roman Catholicism has two chief elements,
French-Canadian and Irish-American ; I fancy
there are sometimes rubs between them. The
Roman missions come from down East, and are
supported with a wonderful generosity by the
maisons-mères in Montreal and Quebec ; the
priests and nursing and teaching sisters are
mostly French. There were, of course, French
missions here long before the railway, working
among the voyageurs and the Indians, and these
are still continued in the reserves and to the
north ; but the newer settlers' West also is
definitely regarded as a mission-field by the

Roman Church in Canada, and the regular missionary equipment is freely provided, notably hospitals in charge of nursing orders.

The Presbyterians struck me as much the most " Canadian " body, as distinguished from French-Canadian or Old Country ; for, though many of the people come direct from Scotland, yet many of the people and most of the ministers seem to come from Eastern Canada. Presbyterianism seems to have a marked unity all over the Dominion, Western ministers having been educated down East and being personally acquainted with Church leaders in Montreal and Toronto. In 1913 three or four wealthy laymen arranged to pay the fares of every minister in the Dominion and his wife to and from the General Dominion Assembly of that year. Such a meeting would do a great deal to maintain unity, but was not necessary to create it, for unity existed before. Money too, I believe, comes freely from the East ; but the gift of men is the great thing.

There is a direct Scottish influence on Canadian Presbyterianism, but it acts on the centres and through the centres. Scottish professors and preachers come to Halifax, Montreal, Toronto, Winnipeg, Vancouver, but there is no management of separate districts in the West by different branches of Presbyterianism in Scotland. Since the days of Dr. Robertson, the great superintendent of Western Missions, the Eastern Presbyterians have been awake to the Western opportunity, and have spared no effort to establish a strong hold, especially on the centres of population—the strategic points—in the West. The Presbyterian Church is most clearly one of the forces acting to bring scattered Canada together. The Scottishness, however, has not in the least died out of it. I thought it very characteristic that the only Presbyterian student I encountered out on the prairie, a boarder in a remote farm, was discovered under a dim lamp, deep in his books. There is indeed one lamentable falling-away. What is the use of a plain and ancient psalm-tune if the assembled congregation leaves it to the choir ?

In two ways at least the Presbyterian Church has definitely adapted itself to the special Western circumstances. The young student-evangelists in the scattered country districts need superintendence, and superintendents have been provided. A wind has blown from the prairie and has given back to Anglicans legislating Synods and strong lay representation, and to Presbyterians an office suggesting Prelacy. But an even more curious fact appears in connection with the Ruthenians. The Presbyterian Church has taken up the question of the Ruthenians, and is working for them at Vegreville, Alberta, and conversation ran persistently on Mr. Lloyd George and the Insurance Act, not a Canadian question! Listening and looking round I realized that almost all the men were English. The needs of English immigrants into the West have been met from England, with devotion and generosity, but with certain dubious accompaniments. It is not to be supposed that English authorities deliberately wish to maintain such a control as to prevent the growth of a genuine Canadian daughter of the English Church, but the present methods of helping do actually appear to tend that way; and the trouble is increased by the fact that there are two or three separate English connections, which tend not only to keep the West divided from the East, but to cut off one diocese from another on English ecclesiastical party lines. A diocese supported by the Society for the Propagation of the Gospel and a diocese supported by the Colonial and Continental Church Society have few dealings together, and the Archbishops' Fund Brotherhoods make a further complication. Instead of being encouraged to try to understand the Canadian mind, and to become Canadians, most of the young English volunteers in church work on the prairie are kept carefully within reach of the atmosphere of this or that English school of thought, and only the stronger minds can escape. Young Evangelicals

are sent out West in batches—to an English
Evangelical College, in the hands of an English
society, with an English Principal; young High
Churchmen are sent out in batches to a High
Church Brotherhood redolent of Oxford. This is
to change the sky, but not the mind ; but the sky
does tell in the end, in spite of all.

Having ventured to criticize so freely the system of Anglican work in the West, I hope I may
still be permitted to pay my tribute of honour to
the men and women who do the work. Englishmen constantly show a fine simplicity and dis-
interestedness in accepting poverty and a very
limited sphere, as the world judges. Many a
brilliant student has spent a life of quiet service
in a country vicarage without a touch of bitter-
ness, and the same spirit is alive on the prairie.
The Canadian or the Scot or the American may
pine for the city. The French missionary pur-
sues his solitary way far in the back country ; but
his English brother is not so far behind him,
either among the Indians or the settlers. Indeed,
among the settlers the Englishman has probably
a wider range, for the Romans try to keep their
flocks together, while the Anglicans make a noble
effort to cover the ground. I saw the Church of
England in her glory on the prairie.

It was the glory of Holy Poverty, not of an
" established social position." The system in the

diocese I knew best was to send out the students
from College to take prairie districts in summer.
One " catechist " might have three stations ten
miles or so apart. The catechist's salary did not
allow of his boarding in a farm, so he " batched "
in a one-roomed shack. Services were sometimes
held in the ever-useful school-house, sometimes
in tiny lumber churches where the funds perhaps
ran out before the lining could be put in, or chairs
substituted for rough deal planks on supports ;
sometimes again a farm kitchen served as meeting-
place. Routine church-going almost disappears
in the Western country, and a man may drive a
very long way to find only five or six assembled.
Here is a striking difference from older countrysides, the more remarkable because the cities are
rather strict in their Sunday observance, stricter,
I thought, on the whole, than either in England
or in modern Scotland. In some country stations
a Church of England student would come one
week, a Presbyterian the next, and a Methodist
the third, and while certain people would attend
only their own form of worship, others would
share in all three. Kikuyu was at least sympathetically understood out there.

Set over groups of these students were ordained
priests, the " drivers," each with a district as big
as an English diocese, and only less of a wanderer
than the Bishop himself. I shall not easily forget

the quarterly meeting of a prairie rural deanery
when the chairman turned on the women present :
" You could help the students in very simple
ways, you know, I mean with things like dish-
cloths. There is not much house-furnishing in
the shacks, and here are these poor young men
fresh out from England! " The " driver " has to
teach his men to look after their horses, to keep
their shacks decently clean, if they should be out
on the field in winter to dress themselves sensibly
and not be frost-bitten, to find their way on the
prairie, to be helpful in houses where they put up
on their journeys, to remember that on the prairie
each of them is just " a preacher," and that above
all they must put on no airs. I saw later what
love might be won by humble and straight-
forward men with something personal to say ;
and also one could guess how a touch of assumption or a suggestion of talky-talky would stiffen
the prairie backs and set up mutterings about
" a soft job." The driver's at any rate is very far
from a soft job, for in summer he has plenty to do
with celebrations of Holy Communion, christen-
ings, marryings, buryings, and looking after his
men like a mother, and in winter, when the students go into college, he is left in sole charge of a
gigantic district—and perpetual driving in a
Western winter, with the prospect of any sort of
queer quarters for a night's rest, and sleeping-bag

and outfit of tools to fall back on in case of accidents, is not a job any slacker would choose.

A certain rural dean's abode illustrated, in a lively manner, the prairie conditions. It was a two-roomed shack planted on a pretty corner of prairie among bushes and wild roses. The stable behind was larger than the ruri-decanal residence, but it was not large enough to hold the horses of the students then meeting, and these were picketed round. Within the shack, a lunch-party was to be entertained, and the papers of the church dignitary were hastily bundled away to give the company room to sit down on book-cases and other pieces of furniture while the host finished his cooking. The lunch was excellent, and pleasantly seasoned with cheerful conversation.

There seemed no sign in the West of anything approaching the American tendency to new forms of religion, though Mormons have come in from the States, and Doukhobors from Russia. I mean that I never heard of a Canadian Mrs. Eddy, or of any Canadian-invented sect, and that the tendency seemed rather strongly toward concentration. Perhaps the mass of French Roman Catholicism in Lower Canada has tended to steady the loyalties of other bodies, perhaps the difference illustrates how a character once stamped on a people may remain constant through enormous changes. Early British-Canadians were serious men—one cannot miss that stamp on Canada as a whole—but neither Ontario nor the Maritime Provinces were like New England in having their very foundations in religious controversy.

Philanthropies out West are simple and near the foundations. There are very few people with time or desire to meddle with their neighbours' affairs. There are really and truly too few ; but this has at least one good result, that there is no overlapping, and every bit of work visibly meets a need. Most of the help that was given seemed to be given by the churches, difficult cases being sent to the priest or the deaconess. There was an " Associated Charities " in each city to act as clearing-house. A marked feature was the strength of societies like the " Knights of Pythias " and the " Knights of Columbus," mainly social but with benefit schemes in connection. I do not think Trade Unions were strong in the small places, where nearly everybody was working at something different from his own trade.

Till 1913 there was not an enormous amount of actual relief work to do, and such charitable workers as there were could be happy in their work, it was so hopeful and effective. Generally anyone could be set on his feet by a meal or two and some well-directed "'phone-work" on his behalf to find a job ; only the sick needed more. The personal touch was present in all charity, and things like workhouses, free hospitals, and other palliatives of misery were hardly missed. Since 1913 charity has been unable to cope alone with the distress in the cities, and municipalities have been driven to the free meals and attempts to provide work they used to scorn so heartily as decadent Old-Country Socialism.

One instance of the concentration of functions distributed in England over many societies is the Anglican "Women's Auxiliary." This society not only works for its local church, for missions in Canada, and for missions abroad, but takes up Mothers' Union work and the subject of moral education. Another is the "Daughters of the Empire" society, which may be found in different cities helping hospitals, helping to teach immigrants English, giving patriotic pictures to schools, setting up memorials of old-time events, and studying Shakespeare and the history of the Province. This was the only studious society that I personally encountered—the nearest men's society was a Mock Parliament—but some High Schools had literary societies. A very remarkable instance of old societies finding their opportunity in the young West is that of the Y.M.C.A. and the Y.W.C.A. Homelessness is one of the very

sharpest problems of the Western city. Young
men and young women pour in by hundreds as
unattached units, and these societies have grasped
the supreme importance of providing pleasant
company as well as shelter for the new-comers,
and that not only for the poorest. So in every
large city the Y.M.C.A. is a favourite club, and
the Y.W.C.A. provides a home for teachers and
stenographers as well as for manual workers.
Besides the provision for residents there is the
" transient " side, and the immensely important
Travellers' Aid department. The scope of the
work is rather different from that done at home,
or even down East, and one sometimes hears
criticism, but the value of the new functions
cannot be exaggerated, as Western citizens
recognize.

Total-abstinence societies are active, especially
the W.C.T.U. (Women's Christian Temperance
Union), originally founded in the States. On a cursory inspection one is inclined to wonder what they
are so busy about, so little visible drunkenness is
there, except in some old-timer towns. However,
a cursory inspection may be deceptive. There is
certainly, compared with England or Scotland,
infinitely less drinking of wine or spirits as a part
of ordinary domestic life—I saw none at all in
the West—and liquor-stores are not planted all
about a town in the numbers to which we are

accustomed ; the "hotels" are very few, comparatively, and sometimes are all close together
near the station ; and men working say in a
street-trench up-town will send one of their
number to a neighbouring house for a jug of
water instead of to a pub for beer. The use of
strong liquors is not, as at home, intimately
associated with the social life of the majority of
the population, but a detached and not too respectable habit. I heard of no drinking among
women. One understands how under local option
county after county in rural areas "goes dry,"
without anyone minding very desperately except
"the trade" and a few habituals. The great
cities do not go dry. The situation there will
perhaps have to be tackled from another side, by
the provision of opportunities for good-fellowship
outside the bar-room.

In the larger cities most of the methods of
remedial philanthropy known in Europe are at
work, and the Canadian vigour and readiness to
experiment compensate partly for the lack of
experienced workers, and the comparatively
small total available at all. Vigorous Town-
Planning societies exist in the larger cities, but
the propaganda has not reached the smaller
places, where land is cheaper and action easier.
There is one institution with an incalculable
influence in England and the States which is

only beginning to be known in Canada—I mean the Settlement, where the more fortunate do not work among the poor as outsiders, but go to live among them and attempt the hard task of seeing things from their side. I heard of no settlements in the Western cities ; they are beginning in Winnipeg, and there are several in Montreal and in Toronto ; but some of them are perhaps rather missions than settlements in the strictest sense. The pure high doctrine of the settlement as we learned it at Oxford from friends of the first founders was not that the rich should go to be missionaries to the poor and teach them, not even that they should go with charitable help, but that they should go and make the acquaintance of their fellow-countrymen. Oxford was to learn as much from Bethnal Green as Bethnal Green from Oxford ; and this doctrine has never been altogether forgotten. Except for this, trained professional workers would be more desirable "settlers" than young men and women fresh from the Universities, intending to take up different professions or positions in public life. The former would work more efficiently ; but the settlement was originally designed for the young men and the young women, to open their eyes ; and so study of economics and social questions, in combination with personal familiarity with the neighbours, forms an important part of settlement life in London. The result is not so immediate, but it may be more revolutionary. This side of the settlement purpose does not seem to be widely realized as yet in Canada, though there are signs of it in the McGill University Settlement in Montreal, and also in Winnipeg. The University of Toronto, I think, is arranging a sociological course. Practice appeals naturally in a new country before theory, but practice is discovering the dangers of going right ahead alone.

PART II

REFLECTIONS

I

THE GREATE DIVIDE

SEEN from this side of the ocean, Canada appears as so essentially a land of back-woods and prairie that when English people go to Canada or meet Canadians they are puzzled and find their ideas in great need of adjustment. The Canadians who speak for Canada, the "upper class" who set the social standard and whom alone the visitor usually meets, are townspeople, and more intensely townspeople than any class we have in England. In England the King and the Dukes are country gentlemen, and it is the right thing to know a great deal about the points of a bullock or a sheep, and about methods of agriculture; and this affects feeling all through the social body, so that a rich man wishing to "enter Society" buys land and does his best often to be an intelligent land-lord. As in the States, so in Canada, there is none of this particular sort of attraction about the country. The fashionable ideal East and West is the perfectly groomed Company Director, not

anything in rough tweeds; and "the best people,"
from the great financiers of Montreal to the store-
keepers of the tiniest town in Sask. or Alta.,
have the profoundest sense of superiority to the
land-owning farmers, whom they do not know.
This fact can be gathered from many books of
travel, and is well brought out in Mr. Bradley's
Canada, in the Home University Library—"Farm
ing has no romance for the Canadian, and the
well-educated man would regard it as throwing
his life away"; and it accounts for the reported
dictum of a Canadian lady addressing English-
women on emigration—" No *Canadian* girl would
think of marrying a rancher."

The countrymen could well afford to bear the
disregard of the merely fashionable ; but the City
men run Canada. This is the difficulty, and it
makes the social gulf a serious matter. On the
one hand the farmer distrusts profoundly anything offered him from the Cities, even agricultural schools and lectures from the Government,
much more pedigree stock brought in by an
Association in the local City—"Timeo Danaos et
dona ferentes." Townsmen, in the farmer's eyes,
are naturally robbers. On the other hand, he has
some difficulty in getting his own views expressed
and rendered effective. A working farmer is not
a talkative or meddlesome person at any time,
and in Canada especially, where country labour

is so scarce, he generally cannot afford to leave his farm. In scattered districts he cannot often even meet his fellows and talk things over. In none of the districts which I visited in either Saskatchewan or Alberta was there a weekly market, with its opportunities of meeting and forming a public opinion ; the individual farmer coming to town went softly, as on hostile soil, and slipped away unnoticed. Again, the Press represents the City (except a few definitely farmers' papers, *e.g.*, *The Grain-Growers' Guide* and *The Farmers' Advocate*) and the Legislative Representatives even of prairie districts are not generally real farmers, but village lawyers or storekeepers. The schools are in the hands of young girls with no interest in politics ; the ministers of religion do something towards representing the country to the outside world,[1] but they cannot do very much. When a high politician is, occasionally, a countryman and appears as such, the country itself is surprised. " He had rough sort of clothes on just as it might be one of us," said a fine young rancher to me, with amazement, of a certain distinguished person.

So the governments do a great many excellent things for agriculture in the way of experimental farms, agricultural schools and colleges, and

---

[1] See especially the Rev. John McDougall's *Rural Life in Canada, its Trend and Tasks* (Macmillan).

courses of lectures in the country ; but they do not always seem inclined to listen to what farmers themselves say about their troubles, especially when their views conflict with certain city interests, *e.g.*, in regard to Agricultural Credit and the Tariff.   In time this may be changed, with increasing strength in the great farmers' organizations, " The Grange " in Ontario, " The Grain-Growers " in Saskatchewan, " The United Farmers " of Alberta.   Meanwhile the farmer ploughs his lonely furrow, very hard-worked, often desperately poor and in debt.   Too often he falls into discouragement, thinks little of himself and his class, and wishes he could throw up his land and go to town ; (but I have met one or two farmers as proud as Lucifer).   The more serious politicians worry over him, but the mass of public opinion pays no attention to him at all.   At a great Congress on social questions held in Ottawa, in March 1914, one morning was given to three sectional conferences, one of which was to consider " The Country," and another " The City," including such subjects as " The Slum " and " Overcrowding."   For hundreds that attended the other two meetings, scarcely tens came to hear the case of the country. We were a faithful few, perhaps thirty or thirty-five ; yet the words of the chairman[1]

---

[1] C. Drury, Esq., Ex-President of the Dominion Grange and Farmers' Association.

were indisputable—"Ours is the more important
task. We are here not to cleanse the sewers
but to preserve the springs of our national
life." Again I was present at the opening of a
splendid new Collegiate building in a city of
Saskatchewan, and the Lieutenant-Governor of
the Province made an excellent speech urging
that what Saskatchewan needed was a higher
education which should not spoil its pupils for
agricultural life, but send them back to the
land abler farmers. Up rose the head-master
afterwards, and read with pride the list of the
professions to which his boys had risen—"three
lawyers, a doctor, a manager of large stores, a
druggist. . . ." There were no farmers in the
list, to become a farmer would not be to get on
in the world ; and the schoolmaster did not seem
to mind.

His justification, and the justification of the
lady who warned English girls against marrying
on the prairie, lies in the fact that farming life in
Western Canada at present is really a terribly
hard struggle ; and apparently in the old settlements of Ontario a career on the land is even less
attractive. " The Anglo-Canadian of all the old
provinces has shown for the last thirty or forty
years a notorious distaste for farming."[1] But,
along with this judgment on the conditions of

[1] Bradley, *Canada* ; *cf.* MacDougall.

country life, there is commonly to be found, in Canadian towns and in some books, a tendency to personal depreciation of the farmer class, which is, so far as my experience goes, totally unjustified. Sometimes, I suspect, it is due to the speakers or writers knowing no country people personally, and being obsessed with the belief that a thoughtful mind cannot be found apart from a linen collar. I can only speak of four or five districts in the West, but wherever I went I found more thoughtfulness, more individuality, more plain good manners, more of a willingness to read solid books through and to discuss real things, in the country than in the town ; and for the most part my friends were not English gentlemen-farmers or Scottish Highlanders newly arrived, but true Canadians from old Ontario. Mentally and physically the Canadian country people appeared to me a splendid stock that Canada can very ill afford on any pretext to lose or depress.

But apart from all questions of personal superiority between the townsman and the countryman, if Canadian girls will not marry ranchers, and if Canadian lads will not farm with their own hands, is Canada to do without ranchers (and farmers), or are the future countrymen not to be Canadians ? That seems to be the dilemma. In Ontario the present attitude is at least comprehensible ; it may be possible to ignore the country where there are, as in England, great industrial towns which produce wealth. We have learned in England that busy industrial towns and a dying country have their disadvantages, but Ontario has not yet had all England's experience, and still believes in " Industries " as a magic spell to bring in the Age of Gold. But in the Prairie Provinces surely all this is the maddest topsy-turveydom. For why are there towns at all out there ? Why do capitalists lend money to build stores and develop industries in that out-of-the-way corner of the world, with so hard a climate, and so little water comparatively for power, carriage, or other uses ? Surely because the towns are expected to serve the needs of a prosperous farming community, exporting wheat and farm-produce and bringing money into the country. The town in the West depends absolutely on the country, and the country must be developed or else the towns must collapse in a few years like certain boomed cities in the U.S.A. Unless the countryman is prosperous and with a good conceit of himself the foundations of the West are rotten. The division of French and English in Quebec and Ontario has been troublesome enough to Canadian statesmen ; but the breach between town and country is perhaps an even graver matter.

II

WESTERN TOWNS AND CITIES

(A) THEIR RELATION TO THE PROVINCES

FOR a student of the growth of institutions all
Canada is at this moment a vast experimental
station ; here communities are being formed and
hardening into shape month by month, under the
watcher's very eyes; and not only do the processes
advance with a miraculous speed, but they are
seen in a simplified form, free from the modifications and complications always present in
older societies. This is true of all Canada, but
there is a certain special interest in the social
development of the Prairie Provinces, Manitoba,
Saskatchewan, and Alberta.

The given conditions from which a new society
is to be worked out are not the same in Canada
as in any of the other Dominions. South Africa's
case is obviously quite different, from the presence
of a subject race doing the hard manual work.
In Australia (as also in South Africa) mines have
played a great part in the colonial history, and

mines draw a certain class of restless speculative immigrant, only at home in camps and towns; even the bush, under the system of large sheep-runs, offered large gains or large losses, and attracted a corresponding type of man. New Zealand and Canada were in the old days the quieter colonies, and appealed chiefly to the "cannier" immigrants; but, of the two, the New Zealand farming suited the more roving spirits, and Canada's severe offer of hard work, cold winters, a bit of land, and a home, brought her the hard-grained poor men who chopped their farms yard by yard out of the forest, and maintained in their villages the old village religion and the old village rules of life, Highland or Lowland or English, as the case might be.

This is all ancient history now, though the surviving influence of that old life is still strong over personal habit and tone in the great cities of Eastern Canada, just as the old New England spirit still keeps its mark on Boston. Economically all is changed, and Ontario in particular is now first and foremost a place of industrial towns and possible huge fortunes. On the other side of the continent, British Columbia has always been socially different from other parts of Canada. Its fruit-farms demand capital, its pleasant climate draws the settlers who can afford to pick and choose—the English gentleman-farmer trying

Canada very commonly turns up in B.C. In its wilder parts the huge lumbering and fishery industries can only be carried on by large concerns employing roving bands of labourers. The Prairie Provinces, and especially Saskatchewan, mainly agricultural, with only an occasional boom in oil and coal, have succeeded Ontario and the Atlantic Provinces as the place of pilgrimage of the steady country settler with enough adventure to take the plunge and go West yet willing and able to work hard to make a livelihood and a home. The 160-acre homestead allotment provides for this class, and from Eastern Canada and the States and the Old Land the pride of the countrysides has gathered to take up homesteads.

Thus a natural selection has given the Prairie Provinces what is probably as sound human material as is available in any part of the Empire, and the fittest to found a sober-minded united stable society, broad-based upon prosperous farming, and escaping the extremes alike of riches and poverty. Both in Britain and the States, these extremes have been of late threatening to play havoc with the old " Anglo-Saxon " solidity and social peace. Almost everyone admits their dangers ; but it has been hard to find a way out. The West has a fresh start, and all British and American experience behind. Could such a healthy society be successfully erected in these days within the Empire, out of men of British tradition, it would be no mean Imperial Contribution, for its special qualities would strengthen the Empire just where, of late years, a weakness has been seen to exist. And it might seem that the time was propitious, for now at last the turn of the world's market has come, and amid the general rise in prices, country produce is rising most.[1] The day has come foreseen of old by the prophet Ruskin : " Men can neither drink steam nor eat stone. All England may, if it so chooses, become one manufacturing town ; and Englishmen, sacrificing themselves to the good of general humanity, may live diminished lives in the midst of noise, of darkness, and of deadly exhalation. But the world cannot become a factory, nor a mine. No amount of ingenuity will ever make iron digestible by the million, nor substitute hydrogen for wine . . . so long as men live by bread, the far away valleys must laugh as they are covered with the gold of God, and the shouts of His happy multitudes ring round the winepress and the well."

Canadians are justifiably shocked at Old-Country slums, at the poor physique seen in Old-Country industrial cities, and also at the apparent dullness of the South of England labourer ; they are equally shocked at the violence of some modern

[1] The war may strengthen this tendency.

protests against things as they are. It is interesting for an Old Country observer to try to discover how far they are avoiding the slippery path down to these old evils ; their experience may throw light on home difficulties, as Old Country and American experience must often help Canada. In this study, something more is now possible than mere guesses, for a generation has passed since cities began to be born in the West, and they are still being born ; so one can watch the whole development of the Industrial Revolution and the Nineteenth Century displayed not in a series of years, but in a circuit of communities ; one can pass from the newly-settled country township, forty miles from the railway, where nearly everything has to be home-made, through the successive stages of the prairie village, the railway divisional point, and the infant city with its great ambitions, on to the city of brick and stone, established but hardly secure, like Saskatoon, Regina, Edmonton, or Calgary; and so finally to great Winnipeg, throned triumphant between the New and the Old.

Logically, the country comes first ; but the towns are more conspicuous and hustling, and occupy a greater place in the public interest ; and their conditions react powerfully on the country. It is therefore not unreasonable to trace first the career of the urban community, from its infancy on the prairie to its full development in Winnipeg. Two questions arise :

How far are the towns performing a useful function and adding to the prosperity of the Provinces as a whole ? and

How far is their own internal development sound and promising, how far are they likely to avoid extreme poverty and slum areas ?

An initial difficulty in getting at the truth about Western towns is this—none of them, except Winnipeg, has quite reached that secure position in which a community can afford to say unpleasant things about itself. France and England can riot in self-depreciation, and all the talk of " a dying nation," " a race of degenerates," " trade going to the dogs," etc., has not affected their greatness ; but the West is still sensitive. If Edmonton discovers that it has unemployment, the cry is at once " Come to Calgary ! " " Invest in Calgary industries ! " " Buy Calgary lots ! " If Calgary finds it has slum conditions, Edmonton is ready to profit by the opportunity ; Regina pounces with joy on any evil spoken of Saskatoon; and the drift of capital and labour may really be affected. Therefore in each city all citizens possessing property are in a conspiracy of silence, or rather unite in so hearty a chorus on the glories of their city and district that no other sound can be heard in the neighbourhood. From all I have

been able to discover I believe that really conditions are very largely the same in all Western
cities of approximately equal size.

The mystery of a growing prairie town is
" What do they live upon ? " There are quanti-
ties of motors and of fine frocks—a very expensive
item out there—there are handsome brick houses,
not large by the English scale, but again, out there
meaning a lot of money. In a larger city such as
Saskatoon, there is evidence of great wealth—
really fine furs, purring smooth electric motors,
elaborate stores, and houses on which no expense
has been spared—these last oddly plumped down
on narrow lots with every known style of architec-
ture jostling together in a miniature Fifth Avenue.
Yet the smaller cities actually produce nothing at
all, and in the larger ones there is usually more
talk of industries than actuality, for coal is not
yet worked in Saskatchewan, and the water-
power of the River, such as it may prove to be,
is not yet generally available—while I was in the
West one ambitious water-scheme seriously dis-
appointed its supporters. Where, then, does the
money come from ? for it is all made in the West,
rich men do not come as yet to settle on the Plains
for pleasure. The only obvious economic function of the towns at present is to act as distribut-
ing and collecting centres on the railway for the
farming community, which does bring money

that so much wealth should be amassed out of part of the expenditure of a poor and scattered district ; for there can be no doubt that in 1913 the townspeople lived as if they were rich and the country people as if they were poor. The truth is that a large proportion of the wealth in the towns was not derived either from sales or services to the country people, or from railway wages and salaries ; and this was easily seen, for of the leading citizens most were not store-keepers or railway superintendents or lawyers or doctors. The Great Goddess of the Western town, " whom Saskatchewan and all the world worshippeth," was " Real Estate," and the " Real Estate men " were till 1913 the men who made fortunes. One gate of entry was wide open, even in the most agricultural province, for the specula-tive spirit to come in. Towns were necessary, to provide for the needs of the " Golden Grain Country." "Here is a railway station—industries will come, of course, right here, to provide for the prosperous farmers' needs—the village will grow into a great city—think of the price of land in the middle of Winnipeg now—let us buy and sell town lots and advertise the future of our town!" Money was made, the fever was catching. In-vestors from England and in the East were delighted to own Real Estate in the Wonderful West. Prices boomed, and riches came to many.

Meantime the goose who was really in the end to lay the golden egg, the prosperous farmer, was forgotten. " Farming ?—a dull affair! Business —publicity—there is the only career for a man with brains! " The talk was all of town lots; not before in the autumn of 1913, when tight money gave leisure for reflection, did the idea begin to trickle through that in his stupidity the farmer had actually contrived not to be so very prosperous after all!

By this process a perfectly unproductive class came to take the lead in affairs and to attract the envy and admiration of the community. A great number of stores and workmen were necessary to supply their new requirements, and an unsound prosperity pervaded the towns. Everyone assumed that the rise in values, and therefore the Real Estate incomes, would go on indefinitely; and under persistent " boosting," prices of town-lots went up so high that town-stores in business streets were inevitably expensive places—hence the farmers' habit of dealing with Winnipeg, where the effect of high ground-prices is partly counteracted by the economies of big business.

Certain towns, of course, are beginning to be productive, having special advantages for industries; in Alberta, there really are coal-mines near Edmonton, and perhaps there really is oil near Calgary; possibly the claims of all the

various towns will come true in future, and they
will become useful and industrial; but at present
the most typical prairie town does not grow in the
natural sequence because there is work to be done,
and workmen gather, and they need shops to
provide their necessities and other workmen to
build their homes. Rather the industries are invited and entreated to come, " because N——
or M—— is such a growing centre"; so when a
party of Winnipeg business men or of Easterners
is expected, all the city motors are requested to
line up at the station " to make a good impression." The most typical prairie cities are " made
by printer's ink," and in their earlier stages they
are fundamentally nothing else then Real Estate
advertisements. Hence the large expenditure on
things that show, so notable in a new country
living largely on borrowed money—the magnificent schools, the handsome churches and banks
and houses, the elaborate stores. They can all be
photographed for the publicity booklet, they show
the city is going ahead. " I tell you, this is going
to be some city." First make the city, and attract
the manufacturers afterwards; the market for
the manufactures will make itself; it is easy and
delightful to live on hope and promises!

The towns are, in essence, big posters to attract
first the investor in town-lots and second the
capitalist manufacturer who will make town-lot

values yet higher ; but the expense of the advertisement seems out of proportion to the general
wealth of the Province. All the costly paraphernalia of modern city life is certainly quite out of
proportion to what production there actually is
at present in city industries ; and, as I have tried
to show, the cities are strangely out of connection
with the staple industry of the Province, agriculture ; as conducted by the Real Estate Business, they are an unnatural outgrowth on the
economic life of the Province. One might think
that at least, wherever and however the cities
obtained their money, they would be a benefit to
the surrounding farmers as offering a market for
farm-produce ; and this is so, no doubt, in some
degree, but in the districts which I know best
there was less even of this connection than one
would expect, for the following reasons :

1. The staple was wheat for export.

2. The land close round the city where market-
gardening, poultry-farming, dairying, etc., could
best have been carried on, was vacant, being held
by speculators for town-lots.

3. No encouragement was given to farmers to
go in for this sort of produce. The store-keepers
of the city, pursuing a short-sighted policy, had so
far prevented a market. (In another city where
there was a market it was in a bad situation.)
The farmer's wife might drive in ten miles or

more, in time she could ill afford, and go to the first store to offer her goods, butter, eggs, cream, vegetables, all very perishable in hot weather. A low price would be offered, which she would refuse, but by the time the second store was reached the second store-keeper would be warned by the first, by telephone, not to go above his price. There were the elements of a combine against the farmers, and the great distances made the latter very helpless. Consequently a great many paid no attention to the local city as a market, and in fact would have been very little affected had the whole place been swallowed up by an earthquake, so long as the railway and the station remained.

In certain ways the present development of the prairie cities, great and small, not only does not help the country, but actually has done it harm. Someone must pay when either individuals or communities live comfortably without ostensible means of support. Capital has flowed into the cities to develop their feverish life, and every sort of attention has been lavished on their progress. Attention and instruction is now being lavished on the farmer, but he cannot get capital easily to develop his important and existing industry; he had lately to pay 10 per cent. to 14 per cent.[1] If general Canadian credit is endangered by city

[1] Saskatchewan Report on Agricultural Credit, 1913.

extravagance, the farmer will suffer. In connection with the tariff also, the town-interest is,
even in the West, partly against the country.
The farmers detest the tariff, as making the goods
they buy dear, and not helping them with their
wheat ; but, though the smaller cities also suffer
from the high price of goods, yet, in view of
future industries and town development, the city
is at least far more pro-tariff than the country ;
and " the necessary development of industries in
the West" at least provides a tariff argument.
But especially the moral injury cannot be exaggerated. The older people cling to the land. " I
wouldn't like to live in town—they aren't my
kind of people." " Out here, if times are bad,
anyhow there's food and shelter, and there's
nobody looking at us over the fence and spying
out how much we get in from the stores." Some
of the English townspeople, escaped from Shef-
field, say, or Leeds, rejoice in the space and
splendour of the prairie. But the average young
farmer cannot but be tempted when he contrasts
his own simple living and unremitting toil with
the motors and the shows and all the gauds of
town. He does not know political economy ; he
has not had his elders' experience of the un-
certainties of life. If he heard of it all far away
at Winnipeg, it might not do much harm, but
when he sees it with his eyes, and knows that A

or B came out West with the same capital as he,
and made all that money with no trouble in two
or three lucky deals in Real Estate, human nature
cannot bear it. And so country depopulation
has begun, among the English-speaking people.

I shall discuss the country conditions more fully
in a later chapter,[1] and the effect of the money-
stringency of 1913 in checking speculation,[2] but
before leaving the relation of the towns to the
Province one point should be emphasized. The
speculative spirit has come in strong on the decent
agricultural prairie. It is injuring agriculture
and causing a huge waste and misdirection of the
resources of a young community ; it has attracted
the wrong class of settler, the get-rich-quick man
and the man who is proud to run a fourth or fifth
unnecessary store, or be a twentieth or thirtieth
unneeded clerk, but scorns the farmer who works
his own land with his own two hands. How did
this spirit come in ? It is the town-land with its
rapidly rising value which has mainly done the
mischief. There is no old prescriptive right here
to complicate the situation. The land was vacant
and open two or ten or thirty years ago, according
to the district. There is now in Saskatchewan a
tax on the value of lots, whether used or unused,
but it has not been enough to prevent booms ;

[1] Part II, chapter iv.
[2] Part II, chapter v.

there has been talk of a tax on any increase of
value between one sale and the next, but the
" Boards of Trade " in the cities have opposed it ;
and even zealous reformers have had to consider
the fact—unfortunate as it may be—that a very
large part of the present city populations depends
for its living, directly or indirectly, on Real Estate
prospects. The present financial depression is
acting and will act, as economic forces do, un-
hampered by human pity, and will very probably
prevent for a long time any further rises in the
neighbourhoods of the present towns. But, as
the railways push out, and new communities
begin, the old process will be repeated—the value
of the land will rise suddenly, the rise will enrich
certain individuals, and the price will be pushed up
further by a boom. Real Estate men are shocked
at the idea of any change in the direction of
municipal or provincial landlordship of all new
town-sites, to be secured at agricultural values.
" It would hinder Canadian development ! " It
certainly would hinder the recent artificially-fast
growth of towns, but I have tried to show how
detached this growth is from the general healthy
development of the Province. Such a provision
would hinder the ups of speculation, it would also
be a much-needed brake on the downs ; and in
these days, when capital goes out to the ends of the
earth, and to its most violently disturbed parts,

it is hardly probable that any sound opportunity for industries would lie long unnoticed for want of a chorus of professional boosters. Rather the great new Canada would still advance, but in a different spirit, the old distinctive Canadian spirit of sober and well-considered adventure.

III

WESTERN TOWNS AND CITIES

(B) INTERNAL DEVELOPMENT

To leave the question of rights and wrongs as
between the Western City and her two partners
in business, the farmer on the one hand and the
distant investor on the other, how far are the
Canadian cities providing against the admitted
evils of the old-world city—extreme poverty,
slum areas, and physical and other degeneration ?

One thing is certain. Every one of the newer
cities has a plan, made before any lots are sold—
there is to be no private judgment in the laying-
out of a town-site, and there are to be no narrow
twisted old-world streets. The usual plan is the
simple gridiron, streets running north and south,
avenues east and west ; and sixty-six feet is a
customary width, with certain chosen thorough-
fares wider (the very use of the word thoroughfare is a survival, for in these towns every street
is a thoroughfare, being a straight line producible

ever so far both ways). In Winnipeg, the main streets follow the line of old trails, but the rest is worked out in rectangles ; only in Quebec, and in Montreal near the docks, did I see the old irresponsible alleys, and I must say that to the eye they gave a thrill of pleasure after a year of straight lines, though doubtless in point of air and light they were deficient.

Another thing is certain. If one sees a dispirited woman, down at heel, with a drooping skirt and straggling hair, or if one encounters a noticeably chinless pallid young man, the assumption is that he or she is a recent immigrant from the old country ; and I am afraid the assumption is usually correct. The average Western man's physique is visibly above the average British physique, and the average Western woman's self-respect in matters of appearance and finish is visibly above that of the average Old-Country woman.

There are strong indications that the difference is more one of circumstances than of race or birth. In the small city of M——, when I was there, the population was probably much less than half Canadian-born, but in all the mixed multitude there were practically no " down-and-outs." In connection with certain home controversies, I was interested to see how nobody is naturally content with a bare living. Here a bare living was assured to every able-bodied man or woman, but the interest only began after that. A man wanted to buy a lot, and to build a house upon it, room by room, as time and money served. In wooden houses, this sort of patchwork is easy. Opposite where I lived were an ambitious couple living well back on their lot, in a lean-to which was to be the kitchen in the house of their dreams; the house once built, there would be the verandah to add, and the furnishing might include a piano or a gramophone—and even beyond there were glorious vistas. So everybody worked like demons; and in the process one saw faces grow browner, backs straighter, and lips firm with a new will. The general physique was admirable— a great proportion of the patients in hospital were strong young men with broken bones, shot-wounds from carelessness, or frost-bite. A death in the City was a rare event, and the mortality statistics were quite absurd, suggesting the Happy Islands of the West, inhabited by Immortals; part of the secret lay in the average age of the citizens, between twenty and thirty, another part in the general good health of the troops and armies of children who played round the little wooden "homes." In this hustling community of 7,000, "the poor" were not a class, "poverty" was not a permanent problem. There were individual people in trouble, new immigrants mostly, or sufferers from accident or sickness. " The City " looked after them in a casual occasional way— there was no poor-house—very often finding some friend or private helper to see them round the corner. I remember the genuine thrill of horror that ran through the town when, one day in autumn 1913, a certain family was found actually starving ; it was the first time such a thing was known to have happened in M——.

In M——, and other towns of its type, it was still possible for most people to own their own lots, and by degrees to build their own houses on them. Rents, in comparison, were fantastically high, and everyone preferred buying. The regular standard of housing space was decent and healthy. The very poor, newly-arrived, could squat in tents or rough shacks on unoccupied lots, or just outside the town on a Hudson's Bay Company reservation. No building, even in the best business streets, exceeded five storeys, and the air of the prairie blew fresh and clean through the city.

Two or three difficulties, however, were puzzling those who thought of the future. Squatting was all very well just now, and it might not be so very bad for a family to be crowded up in a tent or shack while the open prairie lay all around, and the dwelling was simply a shelter for the night ; but housing prices were coming to be a difficulty for a poor man, and what if the town grew, and

squatting became impossible ? Then again, at
present the children could play everywhere, but
no little scattered playgrounds were being set
apart for the future;[1] and no by-laws prevented
building all over a lot. The town was straggling
out untidily in all directions ; a part of the fine
wooded slope down to the River should be pre-
served for the future citizens to take their pleasure
in ; the City was trying to acquire it for a Park ;
but the Hudson Bay Company, who owned it,
could not be expected to give it up for its agricultural value. The noble river below was at the
moment easy of access to the city, but should a
boat-house be wanted, the price of land would
be high. It was " company land," it might be
very valuable for factories all along the bank.
The city should have a centre, its Place d'Armes
or Trafalgar Square ; the town-hall was a temporary wooden building crowded in at a street-
corner ; there was a great vacant space at the
head of the main street, spoiling the look of the
town—could not a square and a town-hall, and
perhaps a market all be managed there ? No, no,
the land was held up by individual speculators,
the price would be prohibitive.—The interests of
" Real Estate " were warping the city's growth
at many points, and perhaps short-sightedly

[1] There were spacious school-lots, which would serve as playgrounds for the older children able to go some distance.

threatening its very being ; for it was partly the ground-price that made the city stores so expensive, and there were dark rumours that new railway works required would not be located in M—— ; the land would be too dear, the housing of the workmen too difficult.

These troubles are not in the least peculiar to M——. The extraordinary distortion of the map of Edmonton by a nearly vacant square mile in the middle of it is only the most conspicuous of many instances of " holding up " land ; and private persons " hold up " as determinedly as the big companies. The sting of the trouble is that the whole was State property, ten or twenty or thirty years ago, according to the district. There is a direct and deadly plainness about some things out West, with no fogging or blurring by habit and use and customary right ; and the need of a stronger communal control of town-land is one of these things. The arguments are written in huge glaring letters right across the prairie.

In the smaller cities, however, in the summer of 1913, there might be troubles coming, but they had not quite come. There were food and space and hope and work for everybody.

In that same summer a careful Preliminary Inquiry[1] was held in a larger Western city (one of

[1] Social Surveys of various Canadian cities have been made, and can be obtained from the Joint Secretary to the Social Service

the class second only to Winnipeg, and one with certain special advantages), on a plan following the lines of Mr. Rowntree's work in York. In the Report, money wages appear as immensely high compared with those in England. A list of average wages in Saskatchewan is quoted from Provincial labour statistics for 1912. The figures sound magnificent; the average building labourer's wage per hour is given as 25c. (1s.), i.e., roughly $50 or £10 a month. But prices differ as well as wages, and it is to be noted that in many trades no work can be done in winter, e.g., bricklayers can work only seven months a year on an average, carpenters eight and a half. A remarkable statement follows :

" A careful study of the cost of living made in Winnipeg places the minimum at which a man and wife and three children can live, according to Canadian standards, at $1,200 a year " (=$100 a month). " Several items are higher in —— than in Winnipeg."

"Canadian standards" mean principally standards of housing, a four-roomed house for a family,

Council for the Dominion (Rev. Dr. J. G. Shearer), Confederation Life Building, Toronto. I have to apologise for overloading this chapter with quotation, but these reports are very important, and little known to the general public. I never found them for sale in any bookshop which I visited in the great cities, I only heard of them because I happened to be a delegate at a great Social Congress at Ottawa.

and preferably a self-contained house on its own lot. The demand may seem extravagant to an English workman, but these " standards " may have had a good deal to do with Canadian vigour and self-respect, and the absence of a Canadian-born " residue." It would be a pity should they be lowered. The report says elsewhere :

" The rent is the biggest item, the rent of a working-man (with a family) being from $25 up per month, with heavy expenses for fuel."

" A working-man may buy a house on a 25-foot lot for $2,000—terms $150 cash and $25 per month with interest till paid for, or $2,200 on same terms without interest."

There is a pressure here to put up with less accommodation than the Canadian standards allow.

A special study was made of the East End, where " the foreigners " congregate. " Of the 669 families interviewed,

> 374 owned their own homes,
> 282 were tenants,
> 10 did not pay rent,
> 3 information not available.

" Water is being installed as far East as W—— Street this year, or in about half the district investigated. Where the water and sewer mains are laid the owners are compelled to install plumbing and connect with the mains on the

street. . . . The practical difficulty is that over
60 per cent. of the houses are too poorly built to
make connections possible."

" Remember—50 per cent. of the cases of
typhoid reported come from this district."

" The great majority of the Germans own their
own homes. A few of them own other houses.
A number of the houses are owned by well-known
companies and prominent citizens."

In the foreign quarter generally " the majority
of the rooms are medium or small, and in a number of cases overcrowded. The ceilings are
usually low, the average height being seven feet
. . . on the whole they are in fair repair."

Cases of overcrowding are given :

" Case A.—In a five-roomed house, man, wife,
and fourteen boarders. Two men sick—beds
filthy.

" Case C.—A four-roomed house occupied by
three families. In each family, a man, wife, and
child.

" Case D.—In two rooms, seven persons—a
man, his wife, four children, and a boarder. One
girl was 16, and one boy about 18 years of age.

" . . . The Ruthenians are the worst overcrowded.

" In the East End . . . the majority of these
wage-earners were unemployed for several months
every winter. In a large number of cases the

income of the husband is supplemented by the earnings of the wife. This often involves the neglect of home and children."

The Report dealt with ground-prices :

" A firm of real estate and rental agents furnishes the following *re* land values :

A. Lots in a good residential location with sewer and water connections run at $50 to $110 per foot frontage—in exceptionally fine locations bringing $150.

B. In a working-man's district on the outskirts, but within reach of the street-car, lots may be secured for $10 to $15 per foot frontage." (There would be no water or sewerage here, probably.)

"C. In the East End" (the foreign quarter), " most of which is ' close in,' property is worth $35 to $40 per foot frontage.

D. An instance was given of a residential street which may become a business street, in which property was sold for $600, and is now being held at $700."

The report mentions many city by-laws framed to prevent bad conditions, but goes on—" the danger is that the building inspector with only local experience should frame by-laws after those of other Western cities, which are far from being models, or after those of Eastern American cities, where conditions are such as should never obtain in a new land of broad acres. A still greater danger is that the activity of 'interested' speculators and builders, coupled with the apathy of an uninterested public, should balk the efforts even of honest and efficient officials. Further, the best of by-laws are practically valueless unless the building inspector is given an adequate staff, and is backed by an enlightened and active civic conscience."

It is to be noted, then, that in this intermediate type of city, in a year of great prosperity (1912) :

1. Housing expenditure has come to bear a high proportion to all other elements in a workman's budget, and there is a temptation to economize on this.

2. Work by married women away from home has begun.

3. The non-English speaking immigrants, who are the poorest, congregate in a district by themselves out of sight of the other residents. Their own standards are low, and the sanitary situation is so far worse than in any English city in that there are often no water or sewage arrangements and none of the streets or yards are paved. On the other hand, there is still air and light, as the city is not very large and the buildings are low.

These conditions at least have their dangers for the future. Can they be arrested, or must they go further? The difficulty seems to be partly in the high price of land, partly in the fact of nearly everyone being too busy to bother about finding out the truth. I have been repeatedly told by honest citizens that there is no danger of the slum in Canada "because there is a Town-Planning Society" or "because the Churches send deaconesses to the North End." The poor deaconesses would be surprised to know with what power they are credited against forces that have swept in the past over many a Parish Church!

I happened to be passing through another of the Western cities at a time when strange discoveries resulted from a fight in a foreign rooming-house. Part of the newspaper report ran as follows:

"In the front of the building was a small store, the floor of which was thickly coated with mud and other filth. Here foodstuffs, cabbage, flour, fish, bread, and other cheap commodities, were scattered about helter-skelter in dust and dirt. A barrel of salt was covered with a heap of filthy underclothing.

"Back of the partition, in a space about 13 by 15 feet, were three large double bunks covered with rotting cloth blankets, and a couple of tables littered with crusts of stale bread and gnawed bones. Sitting about were fourteen unemployed, looking like hunted rats, as Alderman —— pawed his way through the line of dirty clothes and towels that divided the room. An opening door revealed the lavatory. The water was wasting, and had frozen all over the floor. The stench was sickening.

" Downstairs in the cellar where the affray of Thursday night took place, a number of men were sweeping the floor, and a row of bones, crusts, mud, and other filth was heaped up nearly a foot high. Here the atmosphere was sickening, and the only exit for it was up the stairs to the store."

According to the newspaper the medical officer declared he knew of more than fifty such places, " but we can do nothing in the matter, except wherever possible work a bluff. . . . A short time ago, in a similar case before the magistrate, we were asked under what by-law we acted. The case was rejected immediately, when the magistrate found that there was no by-law covering such cases. Yet we have taken every step in our power to secure such a by-law, many months ago, but so far nothing has resulted."

The Survey[1] of a young industrial city in New Ontario, where much labour is required, leaves a very definite impression. Here " the foreigners " amount to one-third, perhaps more, of the total

[1] See page 128 and note.

population. " The most congested blocks are to be found in —— sections, many of which have 300 to 350 people. While this may not seem a great number, so many are crowded in the houses that there is a very serious congestion. The causes of this congestion are mainly the scarcity of houses and the high rent asked. . . . In the block 238 persons were living : Ruthenians 141, Slovacks 36, Russians 19, Poles 19, Austrians 11, Italians 6, Bokowinians 6. There were 158 men, 29 women, 28 girls, and 23 boys—40 men were ' batching ' or ' shacking ' " (*i.e.*, living by themselves with no woman) " and 89 lodged with 16 of the families.

" In the 35 occupied dwellings there were 88 rooms. If we set aside one room in each house as kitchen-laundry-and-dining-room, we have 53 sleeping-rooms. That is, 4 or 5 persons slept in each of these remaining rooms. There were 131 beds in the block.

" There were no bath-tubs in any of the houses. Twelve householders definitely stated that the city had never removed garbage from their premises, and the majority of the others complained that garbage was seldom removed. Refuse and sink-water were everywhere in evidence; 23 of the houses had water-taps. There were no toilets, 23 dry closets were the only conveniences of the kind."

In another block, " one house of five rooms sheltered 18 Bokowinians ; another of nine very small rooms housed 17 Greeks. Seventeen Italians were found in a house of six rooms, and 13 Italians in a house of three rooms. These figures are likely under the mark, as the people are unwilling to tell the number where there is most serious overcrowding. For instance, an Italian family said there were 10 persons in the house, but we found 14 beds, and another with 17 Italians had 21 beds."

" The infantile mortality rate . . . was 238.9 per 1,000 births, *i.e.,* . . . practically every fourth child in —— is still-born, or dies before it is one year of age."

Tuberculosis is increasing ; it is supposed to be reported, but " there were about four times as many deaths from tuberculosis in 1912 as there were cases reported."

" The Health Staff is as yet very inadequate to the needs of the city. The Medical Health Officer does not give his entire time, and he requires many more assistants."

" The City removes the garbage and rubbish. This is supposed to be weekly, but is not so carried out, especially in the winter-time. In the —— and —— districts, there is often no garbage removal for months."

" The City has no housing regulations other

than the building by-laws, and these pertain almost entirely to the structural side of the problem."[1]

But, says the optimist, you cannot make an omelet without breaking eggs. You cannot make a new country and have everything finished all at once. Ruthenians and so on are accustomed to crowding and dirt, and a new city has not time to look into everything. There is a certain truth in this, but not, I think, the whole truth. In moral and physical results, it is one thing to be crowded up with your own family in your own ancestral village, where you have your village amusements and your own friends who will help you in any difficulties, and quite another to be crowded up with three or four other labouring men in a place where you are a stranger, and where every decency and pleasure of life has to be paid for. And after all, the question is not one of Ruthenians and Bokowinians, but of future Canadians and future " Canadian standards." The Highlanders of the clearances who have played such a part in the making of Canada came, we must honestly own, from fairly rude conditions. We have heard of turf huts with hens all over them, and the cow not far away, and the midden at the door. But the Highlanders went

[1] N.B. that all these conditions existed in a time of great prosperity.

to Canada in the early days, and in the forest they raised their standards and became the fathers of a race of sturdy sons. It is doubtful if the Ruthenian labourers of the cities are getting an equal chance.

What about Winnipeg, now a generation old, and incredibly rich and powerful ? The other cities are in the half-experimental stage, Winnipeg has taken shape. Here there has been, I believe, no authorized Survey, and facts are not tabulated, but there are facts enough, e.g., in the report presented to the Manitoba Methodist Conference held at Brandon in 1913 by the Committee on Wages and the Cost of Living, and in the books of the Rev. J. S. Woodsworth, late of the All People's Mission in the North End ; and one can look with one's eyes, and see plainly enough where the development of the last thirty years has led. Here one is really back " in town," in the old kind of town. " Did you stop off at Winnipeg ? " " Yes." " Did you think it a fine city ? " " Well, in some ways." " Why, didn't you see the Crescent, with the magnificent millionaires' residences?"—Yes, I had seen the millionaires' residence, but I had seen other millionaires' residences before ; I did not think they made a town. I had seen the crushed little town-hall, and the poorly-housed University[1]—

[1] But new buildings are planned for both of these.

the Horatian principle was not in force at Winnipeg, neither " Privatus illis census erat brevis," nor " Commune magnum." I had seen the crowded centre of the city, without even the scraps and corners of gardens that are such a public boon in the most crowded parts of Paris ; I had seen the smoke pouring out, with power to darken even the clean Canadian air, though not into a real British gloom ; and I had gone north and seen the far-stretching dreariness and squalor of the North End, with all its differences so like a newish " working-class quarter " in any British town. Here undoubtedly there is poverty in mass, drearily and unhealthily concentrated ; and it is not all " foreign," though much of it is. The hopeful individual treatment possible in M—— is helpless here, but there are agencies at work. I quote a stray paragraph from the Report of the All Peoples' Mission : " Public health institutions and agencies have increased at an astonishing rate . . . the new General Hospital . . . its Social Service Department . . . Children's Hospital . . . Free Dispensary and Milk Depots . . . Hospital for Infectious Diseases, the Ninette Sanatorium, the anti-Tuberculosis society with its nurses and day and night camps, Grace Hospital, Medical Inspection in the schools and the school Nurses, the educational work of the Margaret Scott Nursing Mission and the

Little Mothers' Leagues in the schools . . . reformatory institutions . . . the Salvation Army and the Home of the Good Shepherd . . . Fresh Air Camps. . . ." The list is long; it has a terribly familiar sound. A paragraph from *The Winnipeg Telegram*, about the vote on a certain water-scheme, shows the economic frame underlying the outward appearances of the city: "The total value of city buildings alone is estimated at $108,102,525. . . . The civic real land value of Winnipeg, outside of buildings, is $259,419,520. . . . Land and structures within the limits are valued as a result at $367,522,045. . . . After eliminating all duplications of men owning property in more than one ward, and reducing the whole matter to the principle of one man one vote, there are 20,000 people in the city who may exercise the franchise at civic elections, and upon money by-laws." The estimated population of Winnipeg for 1914 is 210,000 ; if this is correct, about one person in ten is a property-owner.

Down East, in Toronto, the provision of cheap and decent housing has been taken up seriously (by Mr. Frank Beer and the Toronto Housing Company), and careful consideration of the facts has led some Torontonians to a changed view of the rights of property. " Personally I am converted by the logic of experience to hold the view that land values created by communal activity should belong to and be used for the benefit of the community which creates them, instead of the individual in whom for the time being the title of the property is vested."[1] But in Toronto, as in our British cities, the harm is done, the process of slum-making has gone far. Great business towers, more or less on the American plan, dwarf and darken the main streets, and just behind, in the heart of the city, the Ward crouches in its poverty and squalor. Except width, which is a great thing, Elizabeth Street, Toronto, has little to boast of in comparison with any street I have seen, in South London or Central Edinburgh, and there are back-lanes and yards full of hidden iniquities behind. " Mr. William Shepherdson, who made the Survey of the physical conditions, admits that the conditions outlined have been known for years, the Medical Officer of Health having described them in detail in his reports two years ago : ' Our survey, made two years after,' says Mr. Shepherdson, ' shows that overcrowding continues as before.' "[2] In Toronto, at a sewing-class at the Evangelia Settlement, I saw, for the only time in Canada, the faces of women (not " foreigners ") wearing the sad, worn, hopeless

[1] Mr. Frank Beer, "Working Men's Houses in Canada," in the May number (1914) of *Garden Cities and Town Planning* (London).

[2] See Report of New York Bureau of Municipal Research to the Civic Survey Committee, Toronto.

look that I had almost forgotten in the West. The University Settlement at Montreal—in Ste Catherine, E.—has the same dreary story to tell, and unhappy sights to show ; and at the other end of the town there is the same vast accumulation—" We have money to burn."

The women's faces in the Toronto Settlement puzzled me. Why were there not more faces like that, when there were so many streets like Elizabeth Street, and worse ? Then I remembered that, even in Old Canada, overcrowding and the slum are new things ; they have grown up with the boom, practically within the twentieth century. Therefore, there are slum-dwellers, but not grown-up people slum-born-and-bred ; and so there are great strong ruffianly-looking peasants going to their work out of these dwellings, brutal or brutalized perhaps but not degenerate.

Canada is just beginning to be aware of a difficulty, and she will no doubt set her mind to work —and once Canadian attention is fixed and the Canadian mind thoroughly convinced, action follows at once. But for the present it is clear that with all her good stock, and her vast spaces, and her advantage in starting to make her great cities after her mother Britain and her cousin America had gathered such painful experience, still Canada has not solved the problem set to the modern State, " To prevent the slum." And indeed, where everything moves fast, city conditions seem to degenerate with a horrifying speed, and with each year the task of mending becomes more difficult. It is clear to me in quite a new way, since I have seen the stages with my eyes, that our characteristic nineteenth-century civilization necessarily and definitely, in the best circumstances, with the best human material, takes from some of her children what she loads so overwhelmingly upon others. In what makes a man, the homeless labourer of the cities is poorer than the loneliest and poorest pioneer on the prairie. There is far more happiness and far more health in the far-off prairie settlements than in the great rich cities ; only, nobody believes it, and every little town is straining every nerve to be big.

because there is nowhere else for them to go. Perfect democratic equality is hardly to be found on earth, but one is very near it here, where every man is a farmer or the son of a farmer or going to be a farmer, and the hired-man may play bézique very pleasantly with the master of evenings after working shoulder to shoulder with him all day ; and though one man is poor and another has a modest sufficiency, at least air and space are cheap, and potatoes and salt pork seem to be found generally digestible. There is long leisure in winter for the pure wheat-farmer, and sometimes, if he can get them, he reads great books. There is often a real love of the country, especially in Old-Canadian country people who have never touched town-life at all, and in some English and Scottish immigrants. My general impression was of men strong and ruddy, of women grave and capable, of sturdy, fearless, happy children loving the pigs and the horses and the dogs with a natural and devoted affection.

It sounds idyllic—it often looked idyllic—and at first one thought that here was country life really on the way to being successful. But in driving about, one could not help seeing these sinister weed-grown abandoned farms, as well as the strangely scattered nature of the actually settled land, with the great unbroken spaces between. Homesteaders could be heard planning to perform the homestead duties for three years, just enough to secure ownership of the land from the Government, and then to go to town and sell the homestead—to somebody. One noticed that the newer the settlement the more cheerful everybody was, regardless of discomforts ; and again and again and again one heard the tales of disillusioned and discouraged farmers.

Now a great deal of the discouraged talk can be discounted, because all manner of people have gone out on the prairie to farm by the light of nature, clerks and artizans, and gentlemen-adventurers, and farming is not an unskilled trade ; and men who know something of farming in Britain, that soft and spongy island, have expected to succeed off-hand in a country where the ground is iron for five months with frost, and where in nearly a year I only saw " the dykes filled " to my Scottish satisfaction three times, twice with rain and once with snow. Where I saw good well-farmed clean wheat, the farmer *generally* turned out to be a country-man born, from Ontario or Manitoba or the States. A prudent man, who has not farmed before somewhere on the American continent, will take a season or two as a hired-man and perhaps a course at an agricultural college before he attempts to set up for himself.

But even allowing for this abundant source of

disappointment, the position was not altogether
satisfactory. One farmer's wife I did meet—a
great-grandmother—who declared that all was
absolutely well. " Bad harvests ? "—she scouted
the idea. " We've never had a bad harvest all
these eight years." She and her husband had a
decent house and steading, a garden brilliant
with Shirley poppies, a flourishing vegetable-
patch, golden wheatfields—on the 14th of
August—and delicious milk to offer to a guest.
But the experience could not be taken for a fair
average ; the farm was peculiarly well-placed,
in a sheltered position, and near town, having
been located early ; and, even more important,
the couple were of that particular Perthshire
type—I know it well—which works from four in
the morning till sundown, with undiminished
fighting vigour, from early youth to hale old age.
To argue from that type to ordinary humanity is
impossible. Farming was not, as a fact, generally
popular, and many who had tried it spoke of it
with a certain horror. People who came West
deliberately intending to farm, some of them
good hardy country-men, had given up their
land or left it. Various causes were stated, besides
the mere attractiveness of town-life, principally
the loneliness of the prairie and the impossibility
of making farming pay.

The loneliness of many parts is still extreme.

The farms are large, a quarter square mile at the least. In three districts I knew blocks of empty "Company land" were constantly intervening, breaking up the settled country and harbouring gophers. These are lands granted tax-free to the Canadian Pacific Railway Company, as part of the bargain under which the line was built, and they have been held, for surrounding settlement to make them more valuable. The C.P.R. created Western Canada a generation ago, but now these empty lands are a perpetual irritant. Much of the rest of the land, for one reason or another, is not taken up, and in some districts much that is taken up is in the hands of foreigners. Roman Catholic settlers are influenced by their priests to settle together, but the true Anglo-Saxon of other communions shows his independence by wandering where he will. Thus an English-speaking family may be surrounded by Scandinavians or Galicians or Indian half-breeds, and there may be no neighbours at all, or no woman neighbours. I stayed with an Englishwoman on the borders of an Indian reserve in a most picturesque desolation, and I think she said the nearest Englishwoman was seven miles off ; certainly the seven miles trail by which we left that farm was bare of habitations. Far worse cases could be found ; in this case there was a large family to keep things going. But I had an old-timer

L

friend, a sort of mother to all her district, and at
dish-washing time in the kitchen she told me
stories of the prairie. It seemed as if her acquaintance might be divided into three sets—the
" lovely " people, the " nice young fellows that
don't know the first thing about farming," and
the men and the women who went mad. The
prairie madness is perfectly recognized and very
common still; the "bachelors"[1] suffer worst,
and the women. For even if neighbours are not
so impossibly far off, yet the homesteader has
to work hard all day, and is in no great mood for
exerting himself in the evening to walk to a neighbour's ; if he is poor and has only oxen, their
slowness is unendurable for a pleasure-trip—they
make about two miles an hour, and I was informed
that a " converted man " had to sell his oxen,
because it was impossible for an ox-driver not to
curse. A woman alone in the house all day may
find the silence deadly ; in the wheat-farming
stage there may not even be a beast about the
place. Her husband may be tired at night, and
unwilling to " hitch up " and drive her out " for
a whimsy"; or the husband may be willing and
sympathetic, but she may grow shy and diffident,
and not care to make the effort to tidy herself up

[1] "Bachelor" has the technical meaning of a man living by
himself or with other men, with no woman in the house. A
widower or grass-widower "batches," an unmarried man with a
sister or housekeeper does not.

and go to see a neighbour—any neighbour, just
to break the monotony. Then fancies come, and
suspicions, and queer ways, and at last the young
Mounted Policeman comes to the door, and carries
her away to the terrible vast " Sanatorium " that
hangs above the Saskatchewan. There is still
that kind of loneliness on the prairie. Also, with
the country only half filled up, no neighbourhood
is populous. Twenty houses, perhaps, or thirty,
within reach for social purposes, make a good
neighbourhood. Not all can bear such lack of
variety ; and cut-worms and your neighbours'
ways lose their freshness at times as subjects of
conversation.

Mixed farming is not so lonely or monotonous,
because the pig falls mysteriously ill and has to
be nursed, or a calf is born in a great frost, and has
to be coaxed into life beside the kitchen stove, or
a horse strays from the pasture over hill and dale,
or the poultry get up a vast excitement because
they see a white pigeon and think it is a new kind
of hawk ; but on the other hand the grind is
worse. Day in day out, in fair or foul weather,
in health or sickness, the cows *must* be driven
from pasture and milked, the team-horses watered
and fed, the poultry fed and shut up, the eggs
gathered. No holiday or change is possible. It
is the singlehandedness of the average prairie
farm and the distance from neighbours that makes

it all so difficult. " I swore when I came out of Ontario that I would never have a mixed farm again, because the work never stopped, Sunday or Saturday. But here I am, you see, at it still, and likely to be, till I die."

All this would improve if the country really filled up. There would be more neighbours, and they would be nearer. There would be more ordinary sociability, and there would be more available help in times of trouble. A solitary man or a lonely couple would no longer feel as if they individually were up against the whole heartless prairie, and were not sufficient for the struggle. Then, again, if labour were available, it would make a difference. Of course it is economically unwise to depend entirely on one crop, e.g., wheat, but even granted money or easy credit to buy stock, mixed farming is difficult for one pair of hands ; a hired-man on a farm would make a great many things possible. Townsmen console the farmers by assuring them that all this will come in time, and the farmers sometimes cheer themselves in the same way ; and the Governments make magnificent efforts, in agricultural colleges and schools, and through itinerant lecturers, to teach the new methods, which nearly all imply more labour than at present, and neighbours within reach.

But the hard fact is that the country is not

now filling up. Settlers go in, but settlers come out again, sick of the country. The Lieutenant-Governor of Saskatchewan declared in my hearing, in autumn 1913, that in spite of all the new country being opened up the agricultural population of the Province was nearly at a standstill. The population of Saskatchewan had gone up by leaps and bounds in the last few years, but not the agricultural population—and from all one sees and hears one would guess especially not the agricultural population of Canadian, British, or American birth.

The *Anglo-Canadian Year Book* for 1914 gives the following tables of acreage under cultivation in the North-West Provinces :[1]

	1900	1905	1906
Wheat ...	2,495,466	3,941,369	5,062,493
Oats	833,390	1,697,170	2,309,439
Barley	162,557	370,850	522,734
Totals ...	3,491,413	6,009,389	7,894,666

[1] NOTE.—Western statistics are necessarily uncertain. See the enlightening paragraphs in Prof. Mavor's Economic Survey of Canada in Volume IV *Oxford Survey of the British Empire*, pp. 145-148.

	1911	1912	1913
Wheat ...	9,301,293	8,961,800	9,013,800
Oats	4,563,203	4,913,900	5,305,800
Barley	761,738	809,800	857,700
Totals ...	14,626,234	14,385,500	15,177,300

The figures are prefaced with these words :
" The remarkable agricultural development of
the three Prairie Provinces, Manitoba, Saskatchewan, and Alberta, since the beginning of the
present century, may be judged from the following statistics." It is scarcely the most obvious
comment at this date. The development has been
remarkable, but considering the stream of immigration into the West in late years, the huge
spaces still unsettled, and the active railway-
building, the recent arrest in the development is
equally remarkable.

The figures (approximate) for live stock in
Canada as a whole are still more extraordinary.

	1908	1909	1910
Horses	2,118,165	2,132,489	2,213,199
Milch Cows ...	2,917,746	2,849,306	2,853,951
Other Cattle...	4,629,836	4,384,779	4,260,963
Sheep	2,831,404	2,705,390	2,598,470
Swine	3,369,858	2,912,509	2,753,964

	1911	1912	1913
Horses	2,266,400	2,336,800	2,535,800
Milch Cows ...	2,876,600	2,890,100	2,648,800
Other Cattle...	4,210,000	4,093,600	4,183,000
Sheep	2,389,300	2,360,600	2,141,000
Swine	2,792,200	2,656,400	3,072,600

The numbers are not relative to manufacturing progress or to anything else. They mean simply that there were fewer farm-beasts in Canada in 1913 than in 1908.

For the absence of the mixed farm and the hired man in so much of the West, the farmer has a reason ready. He cannot afford them. Stock costs money, the hired-man's wages " eat up the profit of the farm." It takes him all his time to live, and he lives in the plainest way. Even as it is, the whole country is shadowed by debt. It is impossible for a private person, or indeed for anyone to discover the whole truth, but the Report of the Saskatchewan Government Commission on Agriculture (1913) estimates the total debt of the farmers of the Province at the gigantic sum of $150,000,000. Principal Oliver, a distinguished member of the Commission, stated in a public speech, " This year the farmers of this Province must pay in interest on their total debt about $12,000,000 " (£2,400,000). This partly explains where the wheat-money goes.

My own personal knowledge of the Canadian

country is of new districts in North Saskatchewan
and North-West Alberta, where the railway came
through about eight years ago. In an older part,
on the C.P.R., in South Alberta, I stayed in a
small country town, and heard many stories of
the disappointment and disappearance of the early
settlers. "The pioneers go, and their successors.
The third lot will make good." Perhaps they
will, but for real facts of experience one must go
East, to old Ontario and the Maritime Provinces.
(Rural Quebec is French and "solidaire" and
Roman Catholic, and her experience is not likely
to be so applicable to the West.) The experience
of Ontario and Nova Scotia and New Brunswick,
in the Census period 1901-1911, is told by the
Rev. J. Macdougall,[1] of Spencerville Presbyterian
Church, in a book which should be widely read.
There is no sensationalism in his style, but his
plain tale is all the more effective. " Of the 526
townships in Ontario, exclusive of the immigration area—Algoma, Nipissing, Thunder Bay, and
Rainy River—there has been a decrease of population in 423 ; and of the 75 census districts con-
taining rural as well as urban population, 60
suffered decrease in their rural population."
" We may perhaps realize the contrast more
vividly still by placing rural loss over against

---

[1] *Rural Life in Canada, its Trend and Tasks.* The Westminster
Co., Toronto, 1913.

urban gain in certain counties. Carlton lost 2,561 in rural population, and gained 6,587 in urban ; in Elgin, the respective loss and gain were 3,302 and 4,128; in Grey, 10,782 and 7,083" —and so on. " *The rural decrease in Ontario (1901-1911) is 52,184. This is 4.19 per cent. But . . . the rural loss in Old Ontario was 97,124, or 8.36 per cent.*" From immigration, " the Province received an increase of rural population amounting to 121,200 without considering natural increase (200,183). The migration from her farms therefore amounts not to 52,184, but 373,567." Farm-homes are being abandoned. " The historic township of East Torra in Oxford County closed 13.6 per cent. of its homes ; . . . we might specify as well Arran, Culross, Huron, Wawanosk, Camden, Rochester, Greenock, Augusta, Brant, Tuscarora, Kinloss, Bruce, Haldimand, and Abinger, with empty farm-houses ranging from 10 to 20 per cent. But all these are quite outclassed by Barrie in Frontenac, with 25.4 of its dwellings abandoned in the decade ; Morris in Huron with 25.5, Keppel in Grey 27.17, and Sarawak in Grey 45.8 per cent. The loss is as widespread in the Maritime Provinces as in Ontario." In Pictou County in Nova Scotia, which I understand has provided Canada with most of its College Principals and many other distinguished personages, the rural loss is 5,885, *i.e.,* 26.6 per cent.

Instances become tedious. It is clear enough
that if the agricultural population has nearly
stopped growing in the West, it is decaying in the
older East. Manitoba lies between. " In Manitoba the receding of the tide has just set in.
Lisgar records a loss of 7.5 per cent. ; a score of
districts show recession. Were it not for expan-
sion over new territory towards the north, the
whole Province would show decline in rural population. In the East, as Mr. MacDougall says,
" the question is not one of slackened growth, but
of waste begun " ; and the change has come in
the last twenty or thirty years, since the eighties.
" Within two miles of my own home, in a good
section of a good county, there are now fourteen
empty houses which were filled twenty-five years
ago. The school I attended had ninety pupils
twenty years ago, now it has thirty." So testified
Mr. E. C. Drury, a practical farmer, ex-President
of the Dominion Grange and Farmers' Association, and graduate of Guelph Agricultural
College, at a social Congress at Ottawa. He went
on : " It is useless to explain it superficially by
changes in agricultural method. The new agriculture requires more men, not less, than the old.
And don't think all you have to do is to teach the
farmer. The farmer knows his own business best."

It is true that a healthy industry does not
usually require such constant instruction and

fostering detailed care as Agriculture is at present receiving in Canada from Governments and Colleges ; neither do healthy and happy young people need to have their amusements invented for them by benevolent persons. With all the teaching the rot has not yet been stopped—and the tale goes that even the agricultural college graduates comparatively seldom return to the land as practical farmers. It is ridiculous to suppose that Canadian farmers are a lazy race looking out for a soft job—that is not their character at all, as many an English hired-man will ruefully witness—neither do they strike one in the West as stupid or blindly conservative. Mr. Drury has his explanation of the Eastern decline. " Twenty years ago, the social life of the community was abundant and good. We had two glee clubs, one of sixteen young men, which lasted eight years. We had societies and sports, a croquet club, a baseball club. What is the cause of the change ? The farmer has now neither the means nor the leisure. Our Grange members are too tired to come out in the evening. . . . At the present time capital put into farming pays no interest. If the farmer allows himself fair wages for his work and management, he has absolutely nothing left on capital. Consequently, farmers cannot borrow the capital and make a living."

To return to the Western pioneer farming, with

free land and virgin soil, it is quite clear to any observer of the rural life that farming is not as prosperous as it ought to be, either in justice to the chief producers of Western wealth or for the future good of the Provinces. It is also quite clear that anything which brings the scattered farming people together, for social purposes, or for co-operative buying and selling, or for lectures and discussions on agricultural methods, or for united political action, is so much to the good. The social need is obvious in itself, and also if people know each other first, they can act together better. Co-operation and education are also indisputably excellent aims. Co-operation in selling would either get rid of the town middleman or secure better prices from him. Things are moving in this direction, e.g., in some districts women club together to sell their eggs, cream, etc., and on a large scale the Grain-growers are trying to organize the grain-trade co-operatively. Co-operation in buying would prevent some of the troubles about farm-machinery.[1] The governments and colleges urge co-operation, and provide excellent lecturers to explain methods. It is true that the difficulties in the way of organization are great, from the distances between farms, the pressure of work in the short summer, the severity of part of the winter, the "keep-myself-to-myself" attitude

[1] See next page.

natural to country people everywhere, and the variety of nations and tongues among the prairie-dwellers. There are jealousies and misunderstandings between Canadians and Americans and Englishmen, much more is it difficult for these to co-operate with French-speakers or " foreigners." Still something has been done on these lines under government encouragement, and in particular the Home-makers' Clubs—for the women, primarily social and educational—were spreading like wild-fire in North Saskatchewan in the summer of 1913.

But when the men get together in their independent societies, the Grain-growers in Saskatchewan, and the United Farmers in Alberta, they do indeed aim at commercial co-operation, but they also drop at once into politics. They attack the machinery-man and the tariff, and they ask for cheaper agricultural credit, reduction of railway freights, and a check on the Real Estate business in the towns.

The machinery-man appears as the plausible villain of the Western drama. The great firms of Ontario, or American firms with agencies in Canada, send out skilled salesmen into the country districts, and individual farmers are persuaded to buy a great many things beyond the strictly necessary ploughs and binders, and, in the absence of capital, to mortgage their farms to the machinery company. Then the valuable machine is perhaps left exposed to the weather because there is no shed big enough for it ; it goes wrong in some detail, and the farmer is no skilled mechanic to understand the trouble ; and there is no machinery shop within hundreds of miles. In some such way as this the farmer often gains very little and is left burdened with debt. Principal Oliver declares, from his knowledge as a Commissioner,[1] that the Companies do not as a rule act harshly in collecting their dues. " Where the mischief originated was not in the collection, but in the purchase. . . . The machines may work, but often the farmers cannot make them work. The machines are ineffective because the farmers are not infrequently deficient in skill. And the representations made to farmers are applicable to more ideal conditions than exist. . . . Practically every farmer possesses more machinery than he needs. The keenness of salesmanship has led to the farmer taking more machinery than he wanted. A friend of great experience has informed me that in many cases the farmer would succeed if he started with a walking plough and a team of oxen, and had nothing to do with binders and buggies. . . . Credit is a line of business in which the implement-dealer has no licence to engage. Let him stick to his own business and sell implements."

The tariff is at present a live political question

---

[1] On the Saskatchewan Commission on Agriculture.

country life, representative eastern farmers
believe in a connection between the decline during
the last generation and the tariff inaugurated in
1878 to differentiate industries. A variety of
industries are certainly very strong and prosperous now in Ontario, but it is equally certain
that something serious has gone wrong with the
old original Canadian industry of agriculture.

Credit is a less controversial subject, but very
difficult. The policy of the banks, it seems to be
agreed, is to finance industries, not to trouble
with small loans. It is not to be wondered at ;
the farmer is not reputed a good payer—round
M—— there had been, before 1913, a succession
of bad harvests, and the farmers had very little
to pay with. The townspeople, in my experience,
were inclined to blame the farmer as slack and
unreliable, but the townspeople did not realize
the poverty of the country. The lack of credit
with the banks leads to the dealings with the
implement-man, and a terribly high rate of
interest is charged. A very interesting system of
small co-operative credit has been introduced by
M. Alphonse Desjardins at Levis, and subse-
quently in 139 other French-speaking places in
Ontario and Quebec. In this, the farming community lends to its own members, to known men
for known purposes, out of its own savings ; but
it is hard to see how this system could be applied

as it stands to the newer districts of the West where few have savings, and the population is so shifting and the settlement so scattered. An area within which intimacy and personal knowledge is possible would contain, in Quebec, a much larger number of households than in the West. The Government of Saskatchewan propose by guaranteeing bonds to help in the establishment in the Province of a Co-operative Credit Society. Alberta was also acting. But all this was in the days before the war, when capital was to be had.

The question of freight-rates is technical, but of high importance for a bulky product like wheat. The farmers charge the railways with victimizing the prairie, where there is no competition, by charging rates three times as high as in Ontario. The railways reply that in the present scattered state of the West, their traffic returns justify the difference. It is clear that the railways hold a remarkably strong position. Vast districts are served by one railway only, though there is competition at certain central points, and in the absence for the time being of roads and waterways there is no possible alternative to rail-transport. The railway creates the life of the West, and dominates it. A curious instance came before me in a certain small city. A railway employé took upon himself to interfere against the City's action in dismissing its Chief of Police. "The

M

late Chief," he said, " had always given satisfaction to the Railway."   The interference was
disowned at once by superior authorities, but it is
a mark of the overshadowing majesty of the Railway that this individual could even have thought
of using so lordly and threatening a tone.   The
life-and-death power of the railways is in some
degree recognized and limited ;   a permanent
Dominion Commission exists to supervise them
in the interests of the general community.   There
has recently been an important Inquiry, and the
Western rates have been somewhat lowered.   At
these times the three great Railway Companies
hang together, and the other two may benefit by the
tremendous financial and other power of the C.P.R.

The influence on the country of the Real
Estate business has been already traced.[1]

Altogether the Western rural life struck me as
being in a precarious position, the depression was
so general.   Had the harvest of 1913 also been
frosted, I do not like to think what would have
happened, but the good grade of wheat that
autumn put heart into the farmers, and even
when prices went down, some of them continued
to exult disinterestedly, like Déroulède's peasant
in "le beau blé."   But droughts or early frosts
may come,[2] and also Western farmers, like others,

[1] See Part II, chapter ii.
[2] The harvest of 1914 was not particularly good.

find that land does not give good crops year by year unless something is put back into it. A general policy cannot be based upon good harvests and virgin soil all the time. Unless something comes soon to raise the economic position of the farmer, I think there is a real danger that a decay will set in like the rural decay in the East, and that the country will be left mainly to " the foreigners." Far out one finds Galicians in mud-wattled huts, providing for their own elementary needs, and requiring little communication with the outside world. One hears often now of Ruthenian districts insisting on Ruthenian teachers, and refusing English. I am not one of those fanatical " Anglo-Saxons " who count all other races as dust in the balance. The Ruthenians certainly have some arts which the Anglo-Saxon has not—I have seen beautiful needlework of theirs. It is not in itself an evil that the Ruthenians should come to the prairie ; there is plenty of room. But the question forces itself forward, is it well that the Canadians should leave the prairie ? Can Canada, with her democratic constitution, afford to base herself on an ignorant non-English-speaking peasantry, winning a bare living by unceasing labour ? Can she afford to lose the strength and seriousness and diligence and intelligence of her own yeomen ? And is there any reason why she should ?

V

TIGHT MONEY AND IMMIGRATION

I ENTERED Canada on the day in May, 1913, which
made the record for Immigration. Three liners
escaped together out of the fog, chased one
another up the St. Lawrence, and poured out
their thousands in one day on the quays of Quebec.
The following night the C.P.R. station at Montreal was a Babel of every European tongue, with
wafts of broad Glasgow, as it seemed to me, float-
ing triumphant over all. " Canada has room,"
one heard, "for every one of the lot." A couple
of days later, at Winnipeg, I heard the first suggestion of trouble. " Things are not humming as
they were last year, and here are the immigrants
coming in faster than ever." Out West, when I
arrived, all was still optimism, but gradually it
became clear that things were not as they had
been. There was little slackening of expenditure
—that would be to confess failure and to give
rival cities a chance of pointing the finger of

scorn—but there were certain admissions. " Last
year you could place any able-bodied man ten
minutes after his arrival, this year there are
genuine skilled working men on the tramp."

The business explanation was " tight money."
The Balkan War, or the unsettledness of Europe,
or some deep operation on Wall Street—these
made the trouble, all would be well again when
these were over. A Trade Unionist in the cities
might have put his finger on a different spot as
the centre of the disease, and have muttered
something about " flooding the country with
cheap labour," or " exploitation of the foreigners
by capitalists," or " Government Immigration
Policy playing into the hands of the Corporations."
Yet the spaces of the West lay outside visibly
empty and open and capable of producing food
for man, if only men could or would come to help
in the production.

I suppose there can be no doubt that the dearness
of capital in 1913 was the occasion of the Western
depression's coming precisely when it did. Had
there been no Balkan War, the boom might have
gone on a little longer, the towns might have become
larger and more splendid, the country might have
been a little more depleted of its more ambitious
sons. But some chance check to the influx of new
capital must have come sooner or later, and then
it would have been discovered, as it has been dis-

covered, how fancifully much of the former capital had been employed, and how comparatively little there was to go on with when outside supplies were temporarily withdrawn.

Through the summer of 1913 nothing was doing in town-lots ; prices had anticipated the growth of many years, and growth had stopped for the moment. Many a member of real-estate firms wished he had not made that advantageous deal with his homestead, but still had it and could retire there and economize without everybody knowing. If only there might be a good harvest! Then Canadian credit would be restored and things would hum again!—Had that half-expected frost come in the middle of August, 1913, I suppose there would have been panic and collapse. In North Saskatchewan harvests had been poor for several years, and the farmers were near their limit, while the depression had brought the towns into a feverish state of anxiety. Was all the West one huge horrible Bubble, ready now for pricking ? There was some talk of this sort, and probably more thinking. It was, indeed, a crowning mercy for Canada that the good harvest had been kept for the year of depression. Thus modified, the financial troubles became not a deadly poison, but only a very bitter tonic. Money came into the country and prevented a catastrophe; the farmer cheered up, whether he individually got

a good price for his good harvest or not ; and as
the saviour of the country he half-emerged from
his obscurity. Townsmen began to talk about
hogs instead of about town-lots ; but I saw some
efforts to help farming turn out less successful
than they might have been simply because the
country had so little confidence in the town.
Then, in the city of M——, came the first
Farmers' Conference of the district;[1] and the
Board of Trade and the Board of Trade's ladies
entertained the farmers and the farmers' wives.
The country-men tramped the sidewalks and
filled the bank-offices in their numbers, with a
strange gleam in their eyes, as of cast-off sons
recognized at last, but not absolutely certain of
the purpose behind the recognition. It was an
interesting occasion, and seemed to offer prospects of a new turn of affairs ; but I had to leave
M—— immediately afterwards, and saw no more
of the hopeful *rapprochement* between town and
country in that particular corner of the prairie.
In the East, to judge by the meetings of the Social
Congress in February 1914,[2] and from other indications, general public attention was not turned
on agriculture.

Meantime, the money stringency in the world's
markets passed for the time, but the Canadian

[1] See Part I, chapter iv.
[2] Referred to in chapter i of Part II.

depression continued. "Real Estate is dead"—
for the present. I think it is true generally of
the Western towns to say that the bigger the
previous boom, the worse the stagnancy ; quite
small places, centres of country trade, suffered
comparatively little. Before Christmas, 1913,
hundreds of Real Estate men were on the hunt
for something else to boost, and Edmonton and
its "Ad. Club" were out after oil in January,
when I passed through. Calgary, however, struck
first, and seems to have drawn together the entire
unemployed speculativeness of the West. Saskatchewan over the border was no doubt exceedingly disgusted that she had found no Dingman
Well, and had been forced to sit and look on at
Alberta getting all the attention ; but possibly
she may be none the worse in the end for keeping
a reputation for staidness. Apart from oil,
nothing much has been doing in the West ; towns
are not growing, railway construction is not
active, for many of the men in the building trades
who had thronged out there is now no employment. The East suffers sympathetically from the
loss of buying power in the West, and from the
heavy decline in the immigrant traffic. Unemployment was common in nearly all Canadian
cities last winter and the prospects for this winter
were said by good authorities to be worse ; for
months before the war the Government warnings

against immigration had full justification, and the passionate feeling of the British Columbians about the Hindoo labourers on the Komagata Maru was easily comprehensible.[1] We were told that " another good harvest is wanted, and trade will boom again in 1915 or 1916." Quite apart from War distress, I do not see how trade is to have any sound prosperity until there is a broader base to the whole Western economic edifice, which has been, in my belief, thoroughly top-heavy. Even before the war, the headlong activity had stopped, and the outside investor had found time to look round ; the machine was not likely to start off again in quite the same way, though there were plenty of people trying with all their might to get it going. Good harvests now might be of infinite value to Canada, but they would not be a benefit

[1] It is not easy to get accurate information about unemployment, because of the rivalry between the cities and the private interests involved and the general sensitiveness of western credit (see Part II, chap. ii, p. 111), which all tend to the suppression and mimimizing of facts. Trades Councils issue figures, but they are sometimes held to lie under the opposite suspicion, of exaggeration. In Toronto there is a Civic Employment Bureau under the Board of Control, whose lists give something to go upon, and a Committee of the Associated Charities of Winnipeg made an inquiry in the spring of 1914 and presented a report including figures from Edmonton, Calgary, and Regina.

It is hard to say how the war will ultimately affect Canada's economic position, whether it will profit her as an unravaged producing country or ruin her as a borrowing country. At first everything was dislocated, and the rise of prices and the stoppage of employment was felt far out in remote corners.

at all if they were only to restore the old hypno-
tized confidence, and lead to agriculture dropping
sharply back out of consideration before Canada
as a whole had realized its critical situation. To
ensure sound and steady progress the economic
position of the farmer must be strengthened,
whether by lowering the tariff on his special
requirements or in some other way ; and changes
in a farmer's position need time to tell.

The Tariff question is of course a Dominion one,
and in regard to it the immediate interests of the
cities of Ontario directly clash with those of the
farming west, and of the western cities as depend-
ent on farming ; the recent Provincial Elections
in Ontario show the solid conservatism of feeling
there. At present the Dominion Government is
pursuing towards agriculture the policy of education and suggestions of co-operation, while the
Railway Commission has compelled a certain
lowering of the Western railway rates. The
credit question was being approached, but its
difficulty will now be immensely increased.

Can farming be made economically sound in
the West at all, one year with another, for
people of British-American standards ? Is it a
hopeless business really ? and is the serious
catastrophe only put off ? One asks oneself the
question sometimes in the rebound on discovering
the recklessness of some Western "facts and

figures,"[1] or after hearing a succession of tales of defeat, or seeing the face of some sturdy labouring Swede at the mention of the word "homestead." " Go out on the homestead again ?—No! " Yet there is the beautiful wheat, less in quantity to the acre than in well-farmed land at home, but first-rate in quality. Should frost come before the harvest, if the wheat is nearly ripe it is not utterly ruined, or rendered worthless, though it is no longer top-grade. I have seen splendid vegetables and small fruit successfully grown by a family where the father was a gardener by trade and the sons ran the farm; and all domestic animals seem to take kindly to the climate—except that wanderer from the south, the cat. (Sheep were a burning question, see ch. iii, Pt. I.) It is not to be supposed that working farmers would ever in any circumstances make large profits, unless by selling their farms for town-sites or oil-fields and so ceasing to be farmers ; but the question is not of large profits, but of a decent livelihood and reasonable interest on capital. Seeing what a number of the forces at present working against the farmer are perfectly within human power—his own[2] or the com-

---

[1] See Prof. Mavor's " Economic Survey," in the Canadian part of the *Oxford Survey of the British Empire*, Vol. IV, pp. 145-148, already quoted.

[2] One great source of poverty and debt among farmers is the passion some of them have for acquiring more land than they can work.

munity's—to remove, it is impossible to doubt the fundamental soundness of the prairie provinces.

If one face of the modern Canadian situation is the shortage of capital, the other is the immigration. Everybody knows about the tremendous rush to Canada from this country, culminating in 1913; most people know about the drift north from the Dakotas and other Middle-Western agricultural states; and everybody has heard of the Orientals; and yet perhaps comparatively few realize the full meaning of Immigration on the Canadian side.

The Oriental Immigration stands by itself, the undesirability of perfectly free entry being accepted as an axiom. In 1907-8 the Japanese entering Canada were over 7,000, but the alarm was raised, and a restrictive agreement has been made between the Canadian and Japanese Governments. The figures for 1911-12 and 1912-13 are a little over 700 each. The Chinese are present in much larger numbers; they have not only come into British Columbia, but they are to be found as laundry-men, cooks, and restaurant-keepers in every city on the prairie, and East in Toronto and Montreal, and their advance posts have even reached Prince Edward Island. The restriction, by a head-tax of $500 (£100) on entry, has not kept Chinese labour out; the money is produced somehow or advanced by agents, and

the entries have increased from 7 in 1900-1 to
7,445 in 1912-13. It *has* kept out families, and
the Chinese in Canada are nearly all boys and
men. The question is obviously not solved.

Hitherto the entries from India have remained
low (211 in 1912-13), but the Komagata Maru
incident has raised, and was meant by the contractor to raise, the Hindoo[1] question sharply;
and now a more permanent solution will have to
be found than that based on the present overcrowded state of the labour-market. The idea of
"Imperial Citizenship" has given the Hindoos
their special claim, and has had an influence on
opinion in Great Britain. This claim is now
enormously strengthened, yet the question is
desperately difficult. The whole theory of the
States and of Canada in respect to European
immigration has been that, whatever the temporary inconveniences, in a generation these
foreigners can be assimilated and take their place
in a united people. With Orientals from civilizations outside Christendom, assimilation is impossible for large numbers in a short time; not
to speak of colour, the division of custom in such
vital matters as marriage is too deep. Hindoos
entering Canada would inevitably remain a

---

[1] In connection with Canada it is convenient though incorrect
to call all British-Indians Hindoos, because the word "Indian"
has another meaning.

separate race with separate customs. But the Oriental's standards of life are below those of the white workman, and they push him out. Were there strong and recognized Trade Unions and a minimum wage for every sort of work, the Oriental Immigration might perhaps be left to itself, but this is not so, and as a fact the white working-class has receded from more than one of the great industries of British Columbia. It is the numbers of the respective populations on the two sides of the Pacific that make the question one of life and death. There are about eight million persons in Canada, and several hundred million in India. India would hardly notice the absence of emigrants enough to swamp white Canada.

If Canada *is* to remain predominantly white, either the Orientals admitted must be restricted and hampered and kept down artificially as in South Africa, and the future society of Canada will be based on a subject race, to its own great loss of native vigour, and with all the wrong and trouble that an "ascendancy" brings—or else the numbers of these immigrants must be drastically regulated. To this Canadian opinion seemed to be tending, as I cannot help thinking rightly.

But the Oriental Immigration does not make the whole Immigration Question. The Orientals threaten the future, but they were coming in hundreds or in thousands, not in tens of thousands

annually. The total immigration into Canada,
1900 to 1913,[1] was of two and a half million persons. The total population of Canada in 1911
was a little over seven millions, the present
estimated population is about eight millions.
Therefore, in the whole population of Canada,
more than one person in four has come into the
country since 1900. Who are the immigrants?
In the fiscal year 1913-14, 142,000 roughly were
British, 107,000 from the States, 134,000 *from
other countries*, nearly all non-English-speaking.
This last is the startling figure, taken together
with the total Canadian population. The States
have hitherto been the classical example of mixed
immigration, but they never had anything like
this proportion between non-English-speaking
immigrants and their native American people.
A good authority in Canada declares " our
immigration from Continental Europe in the last
ten years equalled 7.7 per cent. of our present
population."[2]

I have repeatedly mentioned the people who
call themselves Ruthenians and are commonly
called " them Galeecians." Perhaps the feature
of the West that took me personally most by

[1] The Dominion Ministry of the Interior issues a small pamphlet,
Immigration, Facts and Figures. Other figures are taken from
the *Anglo-Canadian Year Book* already quoted.

[2] W. Lee, Esq., Y.M.C.A. Immigration Secretary for the
Dominion.

surprise was the enormous number of vaguely-defined South-Eastern Europeans, not only in self-contained communities, but everywhere. In 1912-13 more than 21,000 " Austro-Hungarians " came into Canada, almost 10,000 " Poles," and 18,000 " Russians not elsewhere specified," besides 7,000 " Hebrews " and 16,000 Italians. The most notable fact of all is the rate of increase of the " Russians N.E.S." The year 1910-11 broke all previous record with 6,000, 1911-12 capped that with 9,000, and then 1912-13 doubled the year before. It is as if a sluice had been opened. By comparison the numbers of Northern Europeans are trifling (Swedish 2,400, Norwegian 1,800). The authority already quoted draws a distinction between the older European immigration, from the north, and the new, from the south and south-east. " During the past ten years 81 per cent. of that immigration " (*i.e.*, from the Continent of Europe) " has been drawn from South Europe, from the more backward countries, and only 19 per cent. from Northern Europe."

All this is intensified in the new provinces out West. In Saskatchewan, even at the census of 1911, *just about half the population returned themselves as of British origin ;* this includes Canadians and Americans of British ancestry. About one-twentieth of the whole were French. This does not mean that all the other eight or nine twentieths were really foreign, because a number were no doubt Americans of foreign extraction ; but on the other hand the foreign immigration has accelerated since 1911. With all modifications, it is a remarkable and hardly-realized condition of things. The " Galicians " come West to settle, the Italian labourers, " Dagoes," seem rather to stay in Ontario and Quebec or move with the rail-head. Ontario had 21,000 of them in 1911.

How was the avalanche started ? Partly by Dominion Government action. In the Ministry of the Interior pamphlet already referred to, it is stated that Canada seeks immigration from Britain, the States, and North European countries. " At various times during the past two decades efforts have also been made in Finland, Russia, and Austro-Hungary. At present the advertising propaganda does not include the last three countries mentioned." Steamship lines, railways, and large industrial concerns in search of cheap labour have carried on a more continuous campaign, illustrated by the troubles which arose not long ago between the Government of Austria-Hungary and a great Canadian Railway company, which was inducing too many men of military age to emigrate.

The immigrants were shepherded into Canada, and received and arranged for in the Government Immigration Halls ; then, after the first launch, paternalism stopped, and the immigrant was expected to find his own level. Naturally, there is hardly a social or industrial or political question in Canada where discussion does not lead round to the Immigrant, and especially to the Foreign Immigrant.

To begin with there is the mere question of unity; but here the War may do what nothing else could have done. Previously it was more difficult for Canada than it had been for the States to bring her new citizens together into a new patriotism, just because there are fewer Canadians in proportion to do it. Apart from the "foreigners" altogether the West seemed to me to be in rather a vague state of national or Imperial feeling, what with the English who did not always value the Maple Leaf sufficiently, and the Americans who had no special regard either for the Maple Leaf or the King, and the French-Canadians who did not go beyond "O Canada"; but nothing unifies like a common cause and a common sacrifice, and the French and English-speaking elements in the West will now finally be fused into one nation. However, there are difficulties still. Many parts of the prairie are now Ruthenian or German, and English-speaking people taking up land in these districts have very often given it up for want of neighbours they can talk to. One heard of such districts demanding

Ruthenian teachers, and if the school is not to represent the common Canadian citizenship, what else is there out in the solitudes to do it ? In this connection, one wonders where the sympathies of Ruthenians in Galicia will prove really to lie in the present war. At one time the indications seemed to be that the Poles in Galicia were pro-Russian, and the Ruthenian peasantry under them rather pro-Austrian—but probably they are not a very political people.

It is in the cities and in the social and economic field that the Immigration Problem has been most serious. The foreigners as a class are sometimes unjustly accused. One might imagine, to hear the talk at the time of the Plum Coulee murder near Winnipeg, that they might be inclusively classed as dangerous desperadoes and natural criminals. But on the contrary, by the record of indictable offences they seem to be rather less criminal than other people,[1] and the figures of "deportations, after having been admitted, by nationalities," seem to tell distinctly in their favour. The problem is not one of crime, but of wages and ways of living. Northern Europeans used to fit in quickly, and did not seriously lower the labourer's standard of life. The present

[1] "In the past ten years, of indictable offences committed in Canada, there have been 2% less committed by the foreign-speaking citizens in proportion to their numbers than by the general community."—Mr. W. W. Lee, *loc. cit.*

throngs from the South-East, ignorant, with low standards of living, and anxious above all things to get a footing somehow in a strange hustling world, accept wages below Canadian standards, altogether below Canadian standards for a man with a family, drive " white men " out of un-skilled labour, and themselves live under con-ditions full of danger to themselves and the com-munity. Chapter 3 of this Part indicated what these conditions sometimes are ; and always these people live apart, and of " white " people only a very few religious and charitable workers and school-teachers know anything about them as human beings, or as anything more than a useful supply of power for the industrial machine. It is at least a risky situation, and one unhappy result has been already observed. While the foreign-born are not particularly criminal, " in two Provinces—the only two where there are available figures—in the past three years the children of foreign-speaking parents have been just 300 per cent. more criminal than the children of English-speaking parents." The overwhelming numbers of the " foreigners " make the question one that cannot well be left to solve itself.

Few men can have had better opportunities for inside knowledge of the immigration than the Rev. J. S. Woodsworth, formerly head of the All People's Mission in Winnipeg, and Mr. W. W.

Lee, the Immigration Secretary of the National Council of the Y.M.C.A. Mr. Lee speaks as follows : " We welcome, we stimulate, we bonus immigration : and then we arouse public opinion to the point where it demands that these immigrants shall be inspected ; where it demands that there shall be kept out of the country those who are suffering from certain diseases ; and then we compel those who do come here to live under conditions that produce those very diseases. I ask you, is there any sense in it ? " And Mr. Woodsworth, in an interesting article in *The University Magazine*, makes the same point. " Our fundamental difficulty seems to be that we have artificially stimulated immigration, bonused industries and subsidized railways, and yet have done little to care for the welfare of the immigrant or the worker. That, it is declared, would be ' paternalistic' or ' socialistic.' The demand for a minimum wage or for the provision of steady work for those engaged in seasonal employments is still met by the well-worn objection, ' Oh, but you cannot alter the laws of supply and demand.' What is our whole immigration policy—and our fiscal policy too—but a complete abandonment of the *laissez-faire* position ? "

But, say a great many people, apart from the really bad cases which nobody defends, and which ought to be better looked after by some sanitary inspector or other, why should we not have cheap foreigners for the meanest labour, and keep our own men for skilled work and commercial positions ? That is the shape into which Canadian society almost seems to be setting. But a permanently alien class in a state has always historically been a weakness, even when from climate or other reasons it has seemed inevitable ; in the interests of Canada as a whole it will be very necessary, though very difficult, to see that the foreigners are so placed as to make a sound and healthy element later on in a united nation. And there is another point : If " white " labourers are to become fewer or even to disappear, will nothing be lost, even if each man gets another sort of job? At the threshing season in the West, I happened to be travelling fairly often by train; at that time the country is on the move, and labouring men of all sorts and conditions were in the cars along with and contrasting with the usual commercial travellers. I suppose a feminine eye is unduly influenced by looks, but certainly I know which of the two lots I should prefer to have as my countrymen. When you have the brownness and spareness of hard labour allied with the bright eye of will and intelligence and independence, as in many of these Western labouring men, it makes a combination of which Canada has every reason to be proud. She will have paid dearly for

developing her industries so fast if she gets a
separate inferior working-class and sets all her
own vigorous sons at desks. I sometimes wondered if Canada quite knew what a singularly
good thing she had that she should be in such a
desperate hurry to turn it into something else.

Mr. H. H. Stevens, Member of the Dominion
Parliament, gives one instance, from British
Columbia, of how silently and sweepingly changes
may come.[1] " Fifteen years ago we had about
10,000 white fishermen on the Pacific coast ; and
you will agree with me that the fishing population
is about the hardiest and best that you can have.
. . . We had 10,000 of them that are now reduced
to a few handfuls ; and in their place we have
10,000 Japanese working. I deplore the fact
that this great fishing industry has been practically
wholly handed over to an alien race, no matter
how admirable they may be. Yet that is the
condition of affairs, and it has had this further
result ; it was found that they had no labour
to do the packing of the fish in the canneries, and
so on. Why ?—In the Eastern part of Canada,
who packs and dries and cures your fish in the
rush season?—the families of your fisher folk.
In British Columbia there are no families of
fisher folk ; there is the Oriental in their place.
The result was the further reduction of white

[1] Report of Social Service Congress, Ottawa, 1914.

labour and the introduction of Chinese into our canneries."

In politics, it is easy to imagine what might be the effect of large bodies of foreign voters unaccustomed to popular government, and many people urge an extension in the naturalization period from three to five years. Yet, strong as the arguments are, who needs the protection of a vote, such as it is, more than the foreign immigrant?

Now immigration has been checked, and attention has been called to the subject if only by the unemployment figures. The Dominion Government for the present asks for no type of immigrant except domestic servants. But emigration from Europe in the dark days that are coming will need no artificial stimulus; what it will require is control and regulation, not only on entry into Canada but after entry. It remains true that one of the chief economic problems of Canada is " how to induce immigration in sufficient numbers and of a suitable character to occupy her immense territory,"[1] but the immigration of the last few years has been really overwhelming, and cannot be met with a mere careless " Everything will come right." The need of the moment is for a pause and time to think and rearrange.

[1] Prof. Mavor, *Oxford Survey of Empire*, Vol. IV, p. 198.

EPILOGUE

I HAVE not tried to conceal my belief that recent Canadian history is following the American history of the last two generations with a curiously close parallelism. A full development of the correspondences and differences would demand a much better furnished writer than I, with my merely passing acquaintance with Toronto and Montreal society, and my occasional and perhaps misleading glimpses into the life and literature of the United States. For me only the barest outline is possible.

In the days when my grandfather was a merchant in New York, New York was, by all accounts, a friendly brisk trading city, the doorway to a rural country. The " Brother Jonathan " of caricatures was then the real typical American, as " John Bull " had been even earlier a real representation of the average Englishman. The grandsons of " the embattled farmers " were still in the main the same kind of men as their for-bears. Then came the War, and following it the filling-up of the Middle West, and the gigantic development of American industry. Pittsburg

began to volley out its smoke, and the railway-
lines to gather in to Chicago. It was an extraordinary piece of work, everyone marvelled at it,
and English travellers explored along the great
Western lines with the same interest and admiration with which now they see the sights on the
Canadian Pacific.[1]

Miraculous as the development was, it was not
all " progress." The old phrases lived on about
" free-born American citizens " and " every man
getting his opportunity," and one heard that there
was no real poverty in America because anyone
could take up land ; but a succession of protests
began to make themselves heard that the old
words had no longer any close connection with the
reality, and that, whatever the reason might be,
New York and Chicago and Pittsburg were not
as a fact the homes of equality and effective freedom for all, and that it was useless to expect the
meaner quarters of these cities to produce a new
generation of American citizens equal to the old
in physical and mental vigour. The protests
were isolated for a long time, and some of them
were, no doubt, sensational and not quite con-
vincing ; but they gathered weight, and now the
reports of Commission after Commission have

[1] *Cf.* Louis Stevenson's *Across the Plains,* or the western tour in
the *Life of Lord Russell of Killowen,* with Mrs. Humphry Ward's
Canadian-Born.

startled the American citizen out of his heedless
optimism. But it is only in quite recent years
that Americans generally have admitted that
they had at home the Old-World canker of
extreme degrading poverty, or on the other hand
have been shaken in the unquestioning faith that
the one supreme and desirable prize for a man's
energy is to become a millionaire and the founder
of a millionaire family.

The admission is now made, the faith is shaken,
and the best citizens are deeply troubled over
the results of " untrammelled individual action "
under modern conditions. The States did not
believe in economic interference by the community, in factory laws or anything else that
might hinder a man from making money ; pure
individualism was a more universally accepted
theory there (for internal arrangements) than it
ever was in England. But believers are puzzled
and pained to find that absolute economic freedom (within the Republic) has actually resulted
in some scores of persons possessing enormous
riches, often too great for their own happiness and
for their children's health of body and soul, and
possessing through these riches an absolute control over the life and happiness of vast numbers
of " free-born American citizens " ; while on the
other side millions possess hardly any property
at all. If the full and absolute " rights of private

property " are philosophically defended[1] because a man cannot really develop himself, his own personality, without property, then there is something unsatisfactory about the way in which these private rights have worked out—to render a very large number of American citizens practically devoid of property, and therefore, by the argument, unable to develop into full human beings. Also, the social effects of millionairism are beginning to tell and to be observed. The American millionaire class has been honourably rich in examples of patriotism, public spirit, and self-sacrifice, and yet it would be admitted by most thinking Americans that it is not good for a man to be born to millions, nor good for a nation to have its standards of pleasure and expenditure set by people who hardly know how to get rid of their money.

America has not yet moved anything like so far as England, either in theory or practice, away from the absolute high mid-nineteenth-century doctrine of unrestricted private right, but she has lost her old certainty, and these days of " the Professor's " rule at Washington are days of change and hope ; and yet, after all, the task of the States for this generation is but a difficult and melancholy one—that of ladling up spilt milk.

[1] See the brilliant collection of essays entitled *Property: its Duties and Rights*, published by Messrs. Macmillan.

Canada's milk is still mostly in the jug. Her physique has on the whole not deteriorated ; her cities have not the desperate problems say of down-town New York, though they may be over-grown, and certainly are thoughtlessly planned without sufficient breathing-spaces in working-class districts. On another side of the situation, the millionaires of Canada are still practically all in the first generation, and at any rate hard-working men, sometimes first-rate public servants. The Newport type may be on its way, but Toronto society seems at present even severely respectable, and Montreal is strong on education and art. In fact, the general effect seems not unlike the pictures drawn by native New-Yorkers of life in their city before the coming of " the Pittsburg crowd."

In one point, and that a very important one, Canada seems to have a real advantage. The administration of justice all over the Dominion appears to inspire a confidence which has not always been given to that of the States. Apart from this, I cannot feel the confidence of the average Canadian that Canada will in time have all the States' advantages, and none of their troubles. The elements of the experiment are strangely the same on the two sides of the border, and there are indications of a close repetition of history. Leave out on one side the French-

Canadian community and on the other the cotton-
growing South, as elements apart ; then from
East to West the correspondence of the two halves
of North America becomes extraordinary. With
the old puritanism of Maine compare the old
Scotch Presbyterianism of Nova Scotia. In New
York and Boston and Toronto and Montreal, an
old society with strict traditions has a great new
mass of wealth superimposed upon it, and differing
ideals struggle for the mastery. With new
industrial Pittsburg, compare perhaps London,
Ontario. Chicago has its parallel in the group
Winnipeg-Port Arthur-Fort William,[1] the mart
and the gates of the West, with their populations
speaking every language under heaven, their
sudden irresponsible wealth, their absence of
background and tradition, their vigour, their
possibilities ;[2] and San Francisco and Vancouver alike have the glamour and the dangers
natural to a meeting-place of East and West.

On each side of the border you find history
beginning with high and stern adventure and
continuing with hard fighting and unceasing
labour. On each side there emerges a community, or rather group of communities, mainly

[1] Winnipeg is a very long way from its ports, but the connection
is close.

[2] See Mr. Arnold Bennett, *Those United States*, for Chicago's
awakening public spirit. Winnipeg is at Chicago's earlier stage,
but she would go ahead fast on any line, once started.

made up of farmers owning their own land, democratic, hard-headed, vigorous, " old-fashioned " in manners and morals, and strongly self-reliant. On each side of the line, the Western heritage was magnificent, and its development after a certain point miraculously rapid, and accompanied by a huge growth of factories and cities in the East, so quick that people had hardly time to realize what was happening. There has been the same rush of mixed foreign immigration, the same marvellous making of great fortunes, and of moderate fortunes too. Canadian millionaires do not attract quite the same general notice that American millionaires did in the 'seventies or 'eighties because the world has grown accustomed to millions, but their rise has been as quick and as upsetting to the old ways of the country.

The result has been in both cases that in a country whose social and economic ideas fit a farmer working on his own land and independent of all the world, there rises a complicated industrial system with its familiar features—the ownership of all the plant of a concern by an individual or a company distinct from the people who work the plant, and the dependence of the labourers on the capitalist or capitalists for the very opportunity to work. The comparative scarcity of labour is supposed to prevent and sometimes does prevent European evils ; but one

o

The more violent type of labour dispute is well-known in the States, and may come to be prevalent in Canada. The remoteness of certain industrial districts, the lack of sufficient supervision, the gangs of men of every nation, are the same in both countries. Nanaimo,[1] British Columbia, is a name that may stand in Canadian histories. For many months there was obstinate trouble there, " almost amounting to a state of civil war." Scraps appeared in the newspapers from time to time—" riots," " use of the military," and so on. One thought of the strikers as perhaps unruly Lithuanians ; but I was told by an independent witness that these furious characters were mostly British miners, demanding the recognition of a union.

In late years those who wish to improve industrial conditions in the States have had two aims, partly to provide safeguards, *e.g.*, for child-labour, but still more to break the overwhelming political and economic power of " The Corporations." As to this last, I am in no position to judge whether great companies in Canada do actually abuse their power, either in business or in politics, or are inclined to abuse it ; but it is staringly plain that great companies exist and

[1] For the special conditions of British Columbia see a paper by Prof. G. C. Pidgeon, Vancouver, in the Report of the Social Service Congress, Ottawa, 1914.

have a giant's strength. The West is absolutely
at the mercy of the railways, as over huge
stretches of country there is no competition and
no other means of traffic or transit. There is a
Government Commission over them, but they are
so dominatingly important, and the C.P.R., at
least, is so rich both in money and land that the
Commission is not likely to meddle more than it
can help. Again, certain machinery firms seem
to overshadow the whole West, with the indis-
pensable machinery they sell and the mortgages
they hold over land ; down East the chiefs of
these firms benefit Universities[1] and lead society
—no Feudal System could confer a stronger
position. A few such Companies are so big in
comparison with the general wealth of the
country that it would hardly be matter for
wonder if Canada had a worse Corporation
Problem before her some years hence than the
States have at present.

Such a position can only be tolerably safe for
the nation as a whole if there is constant and
sharp-eyed public surveillance to protect especially the comparatively defenceless foreigners and
to guard against abuse of great power. The price of
liberty was always eternal watchfulness, and many

---

[1] But so far as I know there are no new Universities in Canada
created by a single donor. Each Western Province has its public
Provincial University.

Americans believe now that they have not been watchful enough in the past. In Western Canada it is easy to see how specially difficult watchfulness is in a new country. Every individual is so busy, making his own way, or even gallantly attempting to overtake the work of his own department of public service ; and it is so very much easier to say " Politics are a dirty job, I won't touch them." Here again, I saw nothing of the inside of politics and can form no judgment whether Canadian politics are or are not as a fact particularly " dirty." But whether or no there is ingrained dirt there is a deplorable amount of mud flying about. The unoriginal sort of politician that in England calls an opponent " Traitor!" says " Grafter!" or " Boodler!" in Canada ; and from the galleries of a certain Provincial Legislature, I saw one party respond to the most circumstantial and definite charges of corruption, not with any disclaimer or appeal to the courts, but with the most cheerful and naïve " You're another." Decent men in politics dislike this sort of talk, even if they know it is partly a convention like some of the charges in Latin political oratory, and a number of superior persons find in it an excuse for standing aside, and letting things go as they will. They trust to Canada's happy star ; but it seems a strange optimism with the municipal histories say of New York and other cities

individuals, faithful readers of *Cotton's Weekly* ;
while an able and widely-read farmers' paper had
at any rate a strong Socialist tendency, and
declared that there was not a penny to choose
between the two old parties.

In manufacturing Ontario the position is
naturally more developed.[1] Here a " proletariat "
really exists, living in hired dwellings with practically no property of its own, and ever-conscious
of the outward signs and inward power of the
great wealth overshadowing it. The British
working men immigrants take, I understand, a
great part in the working-class movement, which
impresses one as dogged and not negligible. Its
expression in journalism is sober in tone and
rouses no unnecessary antagonisms. For instance,
the men in charge down here are conscious how
greatly the Churches might help in a gradual and
peaceful social change, so there is no old-fashioned
" Down with the Church " propaganda. So far
the Labour men have secured certain notable
successes in Municipal politics, but in Provincial
and Dominion affairs Ontario remains strenuously
Conservative.

Thus the old secure social and political Idea of
Canada is threatened by low subterranean
rumblings ; but also high up in the sunshine,

[1] While the agricultural side of the economic difficulty was less
generally understood. C*f* Part II, chap. i, page 36 and chap. v, p. 171.

where the universities are and the city experts, there are signs of change and disintegration. The chief influence has come, naturally, from the States, where the problems were so much the same. The enormous house-cleaning or at least house-up-turning of this century in the States, the various Commissions of Inquiry and the last Presidential Campaign, have set the more thoughtful Canadians wondering how things are with their own cities and institutions. On Town-Planning the first strong impression came, I think, from this country through Mr. Vivian's tour, but conferences of Canadian city commissioners with American experts have widened interest and made many public men realize the need of a stronger public spirit or " civic conscience." " We've skimmed off a good deal of the cream these years, and now it will take all the good citizens hard at it to make Canada as fine a country as she ought to be."—I heard that remark in the West, but it was a solitary utterance. The vast majority out there believed that things in Canada go right of themselves. Down East the movement of thought had gathered momentum, and the first Dominion Social Service Congress[1] was interesting not only from the singular variety of views expressed on all

[1] See Report, published by the Social Service Council of Canada, Toronto.

manner of subjects, or from the distinction of some of the speakers, but chiefly from the immense popular interest taken in it. Day by day the hall's wings and galleries were as full as they would hold, night by night a large overflow meeting was crowded. The Canadian Public was asking questions, and listening in a very puzzled way to the variety of answers.

Now our period has come to its end in earthquake and storm, and in Canada as all over the Empire class-divisions disappear in the united stand for the Empire's safety and honour. A splendid spirit is roused, and we all try to serve the Commonweal. The past seems to have been whirled away from us, the future is veiled. It is possible to hope that in these great days certain obstinate old questions may solve themselves and the nations may emerge strengthened. But there is no place for easy confidence. The States, too, had their long War, and rose in it to splendid heights of self-devotion, yet the following generations allowed the Trusts to threaten political freedom and the blight of extreme poverty and riches to threaten the very life of the people. War does not solve such questions. But a war like this may produce a spirit in which, with hard thought and patient sacrifice, they may be solved—so far as mortal men can solve them, for a time.

Notes on Sources to the Spectra Introduction

The quotation from Kenneth McNaught on p. ix comes from his biography of J. S. Woodsworth, *A Prophet in Politics* (University of Toronto Press, 1959), p. 54.

The passage from Nellie McClung quoted on p. xxiv can be found on p. 182 of the 1946 Thomas Allen edition of *The Stream Runs Fast*.

Beatrice Parlby's account of the origins of the U.F.W.A. comes from p. 77 of *Pioneers and Progress*. For other accounts of the formation and significance of the U.F.W.A., see Eva Carter's *History of Organized Farm Women of Alberta* [1955] L. A. Wood, *A History of the Farmers Movements in Canada* (1924; rpt. 1975), pp. 296-99; and Catherine Cleverdon, *The Woman Suffrage Movement in Canada* (1950; rpt. 1974), pp. 70-71.